KROMA

bruce zachary

EXPLORING **GOD**
BEYOND **BLACK AND WHITE**

KROMA

EXPLORING **GOD**
BEYOND **BLACK AND WHITE**

WWW.KROMABOOK.COM

Fruitful Life Publishing
380 Mobil Avenue
Camarillo, California 93010
Phone (805) 384-1182
Electronic Mail: info@cccamarillo.com

ISBN: 978-1-59751-042-4
Cover design and page layout — Eric Hoekendorf
Print preparation — Slechta Graphics

CONTENTS

AUTHOR'S **NOTE**

I never had a desire to meet God – the whole idea sounded pretty frightening to me. I never thought about reading the Bible. I knew it was available in hotels, and was a bestseller, but I assumed it was merely an exhausting list of "Thou shall not(s)" and that didn't entice me. All that changed when I realized that it was God's story, not a fairytale, but an epic love story. I don't recall exactly how or when I made that discovery, but I wish I had learned that truth earlier in life. Everyone has a story, and so does God. The reason that we love story is because God loves to communicate through them. What if God wanted to draw us closer through stories, would you want to explore the idea?

I love to look at old black and white or sepia-tone photos. One of my favorites shows some of my relatives on the boardwalk in Atlantic City in the 1930s. The boardwalk is crowded with pedestrians, presumably a summer day, and the men have suits, the ladies have long dresses, and they are all wearing hats. For a time, I actually believed their world was void of color. I'd ask some other relatives who the people in the photo were, and they would tell me their names. Then I figured that I *knew* them. I didn't really know them, or their life story, just their names and what they looked like in a moment of time. I was related, but I wasn't connected.

That's what I had done with God. I managed to get a correct I.D., assumed I knew Him, and removed all the color from the picture. Reduced everything to black and white everything tidy and figured out. Yet, there was no connection. I've discovered that connection, community and relationship occur with God and others when I learn their story, and reveal my heart to them. Real satisfaction flows from exploring beyond black and white, and discovering the many beautiful, brilliant, and often subtle colors that characterize a life worth living.

One of the most important lessons that I hope to carry into the next chapter of my life, has been discovered along this journey ...

CHAPTER ONE

THE DIVER

[HAVE YOU EVER WANTED TO
GO DEEPER IN A RELATIONSHIP?]

BLACK **AND WHITE LIKE SHAMU**

Have you ever wanted to go deeper in a relationship? I was looking at my Sea World admission ticket, reflecting on a recent family trip to San Diego. San Diego is a great town for tourism, and Sea World is a must. I've heard it said that one visit can change your life; I'm not sure, but it's worth the price of admission.

As I stared at the image of Shamu, I tried to imagine what it would be like to enter the aquarium with him. The more I reflected, the more it reminded me about beginning a relationship with God, going deeper, and seeing there's more to God than black and white.

There on the ticket is the blue and yellow Sea World logo, unnoticeable in the picture. The picture shows a scene that occurs regularly in the enormous aquarium tank that holds an ocean of saltwater that is the home of orcas, giant killer whales. The image shows the light glimmering just above the water. The hues gently fade from baby blue, to royal, to cobalt blue, providing a contrast for the main subjects of the breathtaking image.

The picture is dominated by an image of a female diver and another subject, seemingly as large as the ocean itself. He is mysterious (he may even be a she, but gender is the least of the mysteries). The world knows him as Shamu. The name itself seems mysterious, like one of those Native American names that was first uttered around a fire in the Pacific Northwest by an elder of an indigenous group to wide-eyed listeners, listeners mesmerized by the hushed tones in which the name was uttered into existence ... *Shamu.*

There is Shamu, an apex predator, at the top of the food chain. Perhaps the most dominant predator on the planet, and he looks surprisingly gentle ... it is this juxtaposition that draws us to the scene. Here, we see a deadly predator, able to consume an adult seal in a single bite, yet we yearn to be closer to him. There is a reverence and a fear that is bred by this revelation, even disdain. Seals are cute, and we imagine them like puppies. We dislike the orca's diet, but we are awed by its majestic quality. It is this sense of power, and the capacity to completely dominate, that provides a distant background for the picture.

The picture beckons viewers to replace the anonymous diver by inserting themselves in the scene. Imagine diving into the cold saltwater and descending deep. As your body adjusts to the water temperature, Shamu approaches. He seems to take your breath away, which is especially disconcerting since you are holding your breath and have no oxygen tank.

His mouth rises toward the surface. You know he's a mammal, who requires oxygen, but intuitively you know he can hold his breath longer than you. Yet, none of that matters right now as he rises toward you and the surface. His smooth glistening white belly seems to go on forever, like a road trip across Texas. And like Texas, the giant's size is undeniable and awe-inspiring, presumably more than Texas.

You are no longer viewing a wallet-sized photo, but you are now within your arm's reach of a killer whale named Shamu. As he glides through the water and presents himself to you, he extends his pectoral fins like arms ready to embrace. Your mind begins to race, quickly calculating your options like a chess player preparing to move his knight before he depresses the timer on the tournament clock. Will Shamu crush you? Will he gently caress and release? Will he hug and hold, killing as he tries to love you, but keeping you from ascending to the surface to fill your lungs with life-giving air? You want to reach, hug and embrace. There is a longing, but also a fear. What to do? Would you get in?

Many people think that beginning a relationship with God is like getting in the tank with Shamu. There is the sense of mystery, grandeur, excitement, and respect. The thought of starting a relationship with God is also often frightening, but the excitement and anticipation can send more adrenaline coursing through your veins than a swim with Shamu.

GETTING IN

My friend, Lee, would surely embrace Shamu. Lee and I were housemates one summer in college. We lived in a beachfront home in Malibu which belonged to his parents. His dad was an anesthesiologist in Beverly Hills, and he planned to one day level the "cottage" and build his dream house.

Our neighbor to the south was singer and songwriter Joni Mitchell. She was often the voice and conscience of a generation along with others like Jackson Browne and Neil Young. Her "Court and Spark" record, tape, and later, CD and iPod download, were played so many times, that every word to every song has been embedded in my memory. I never heard them played by Joni, and I don't recall Lee playing them, but I played those songs repeatedly. People like me, who are searching, are drawn to deep lyrics. We like poignant words that communicate a sense of angst that seems so familiar. The angst that gnaws at the soul like the feeling of picking up cactus with bare hands, a feeing that remains so elusive and indescribable, but you know it when you feel it.

That's how Joni's lyrics are, deep like the Pacific that she often pondered, something beyond full comprehension, never really contained, and relentless in its ability to ultimately reduce mountains to piles of sand. Joni would stare at the sea: the pelicans gliding in formation like fighter pilots on a mission, the gulls hovering on the breeze, and the waves, rhythmic and inspiring. Joni was deep like the Pacific itself. It seemed there were parts of her that were too deep to even explore — mysterious. One could not help but feel superficial in her presence, or at least I did.

Our neighbor to the north was Kate Jackson, of "Charlie's Angels" fame. She was the "smart angel" but she seemed more like a sea otter, playful and seemingly superficial. She would occasionally come over to borrow gin. She spoke with a slight Southern drawl and was beautiful to behold. Joni's undeniable beauty was less supermodel than Kate's, and the depth of her soul was radiant. Kate was likely more physically spectacular, but the California beaches of Malibu, Zuma, Santa Monica, and Venice were full of displays of physical beauty. Even with inflation, beautiful women were a dime a dozen. Seeing Kate made me feel less superficial, almost like I had a capacity for depth.

Lee was right between the two. He loved the sea; I merely liked it. In the living room, there was a big saltwater aquarium (Lee's). There were colorful fish in hues that only God could create, in colors beyond the "Crayola 64" box. There in the back of the tank was the "diver guy" with his golden helmet and ascending bubbles. He was the guardian and observer of all the fish in the tank.

In a certain sense, I *wanted* to be the diver dude, but that's who Lee *was*. He could sail a catamaran, a sailboat, and presumably a tall sailing ship. He was also a diver. He would catch lobster, not with a trap, like a Maine fisherman in a yellow slicker, but with a spear gun. One day, I watched him walk up the sand with a lobster that weighed over 7 pounds suspended from his spear (the biggest crustacean I've ever seen).

Lee's typical uniform was Levi's 501s, a white button-down, Birkenstock's, and bandana (generally blue). One year for his birthday, we had a "Dress like Lee" party. Everyone came dressed like Lee, a sea of guys and gals in his uniform. Lee could play like an otter, drink like a fish, and could also submerge like a submarine to explore depth of soul. He wrote poetry, read novels, and went to art shows. He seemed to know exactly who he was and what he wanted to be.

I, on the other hand, was searching, trying to fill a hole that seemed as big as the Pacific. It was at this house that I painfully discovered that drugs, alcohol, and relationships, regardless of quantity or diversity, could not fill the hole. By the time I had reached my early twenties I presumably would have been voted most likely to be incarcerated, institutionalized, or identified at a morgue. Not the typical honors bestowed in most yearbooks. I was definitely searching for something but didn't know what it was or where to find it.

Lee would undoubtedly get in the tank with Shamu. There are certain people who are adventurers. They are seemingly fearless: they skydive, scuba dive, and race motorcycles. They perhaps never learned to be afraid of things that the rest of us "rational people" avoid (but many actually long to do). Interestingly, that sense of adventure, fearlessness, or courage may not be faith. It's like when you drive a two-lane road in the Midwest. People wave at you, not like a one-finger wave like people in Southern California, but a wave that conveys "howdy." That wave is often simply politeness, not necessarily communicating any emotion.

Beginning a relationship with God, getting in so to speak, is not about being fearless but it's about faith: trusting that God is for you and not against you. A relationship with God requires the simple faith to learn and believe that God truly loves you and wants a relationship with you.

It's a subtle but insightful nuance. Sometimes fearlessness has nothing to do with faith. Faith can be ethereal, nebulous, and difficult to describe, like buttermilk skies to a blind man. Faith is a declaration of dependence upon God, an attitude of dependence with actions of obedience.

I'm not fearless. There are plenty of things that frighten me. While getting into an aquarium with Shamu sounds exciting, it seems beyond my comfort zone. Nevertheless, my life doesn't seem to be any worse for not pursuing an encounter with Shamu. On the other hand I did have enough faith that I was willing to begin a relationship with God. The depth of God is surely beyond my full explanation. The part that I have explored, that God has revealed, has been an awesome adventure. I'm certain that I've discovered a relationship with God and a life worth living.

I have no regrets about getting in. By getting in I finally discovered what is supposed to fill the hole inside of me. I learned the way to fill the hole was to simply allow God to come into my life. If there is nothing in the world that can satisfy me, there must be something beyond, that's worth exploring and discovering. That's how my relationship with God has been. When I began to explore all that God is, it was like snorkeling. It was something I always desired but didn't know how to attain. I would stare at our big saltwater aquarium, and want to "get inside" like the cool little diver guy, but that was impossible. I was trying to fill the hole inside of me with drugs, alcohol, and relationships, but nothing filled the hole. It was like trying to fill a bathtub with the drain open. Yet, the way to see the tropical fish, up close and personal, was relatively obvious: go snorkel a coral reef. The way to "get in" or begin a relationship with God is to learn about Him, and ask God to be part of your life.

GOING **DEEPER**

I used to love to stare at the fish tank in Malibu. I'd imagine the diver guy with all the tropical fish swimming about. How I wanted to be that guy. One year, I got to go to Hawaii, and I naturally went snorkeling. It was remarkable to explore the coral reef with all the tropical fish, swimming with giant sea turtles, and watching an eel peer from a crevice. Later that day, I met a man who went scuba diving for the first time. He saw a whale, not Shamu, but even bigger, one of the gentle plankton-feeding ones, within 20 feet of him. All the other divers on the trip with him were experienced divers, and they had never seen a whale. Talking with him made me jealous, and I wanted to go deeper. I, too, wanted to go from snorkeling on the surface to scuba diving below.

Later that week, I explored the sea in a submarine, 150 feet below the surface. We saw sharks, and schools of huge fish. A totally different world than anything I experienced or imagined, and definitely worth exploring.

What I've learned is that I can keep discovering more, and go deeper with God. As I read (and re-read) the Bible and share with others in their journey, I'm so excited to keep exploring more about God and His love for me. I've also figured out that, like the ocean, I'll never explore all that God is. That's one of the many things about God that is so wonderful to me. Going deeper implies getting beneath the surface and developing an authentic relationship with God. It means discovering that there is more to God than religion or a list of rules: do this, and don't do that. Going deeper conveys growing in my understanding of His love for me. When you begin to appreciate and appropriate God's love, there is peace, comfort and security.

When I lived in Malibu, an earthquake trembled through Southern California. Much of the water and several of the fish were thrown out of the aquarium. Not the diver dude, he wasn't moved by the tsunami that struck his world. He was securely fastened to the rock - shaken but not stirred. I learned many life lessons from the diver guy. When I'm fastened to God, I'm going to be fine in the midst of the storms of life. I won't get a free ride, or a guarantee that my life will be smooth sailing, but my life will stand firm,and I will not be moved. As I went deeper in my relationship with God, I realized I, too, had become securely fastened to Him.

The Sea World ticket also paints another dynamic picture. Despite the delicate and subtle shades of blue, the picture is dominated by black and white, so much so that our eye tends to ignore the color. That's how we like to approach God: reduced to black and white, everything tidy and figured out. We tend to imagine God as monochromatic: having only one color or colorless. To open the Bible, your heart, your mind and to meet God has plenty of black and white, but it is painted against a backdrop of many subtle shades of color. Too many people have missed the color, because of the focus on the black and white. As you go deeper you discover God beyond black and white and enjoy the relationship in full color.

One of my heroes of the Bible is Mary, the sister of Lazarus and Martha. I think that perhaps as much as anyone else in the Bible she went deep with God. One day Jesus came to their home [Luke 10:38-42]. Martha was the task-oriented sister, and it is easier for me to identify with her. Martha was getting really upset. She was working hard trying to serve Jesus. Presumably she was cooking and cleaning her fingers to the bone – very noble. Meanwhile, her seemingly lazy sister Mary, the relationship-oriented one, simply sat around listening to Jesus. Finally, Martha was ready to blow a gasket, and asked Jesus why He didn't care and to tell Mary to help her. I'm sure she was surprised by Jesus' answer, "Martha, Martha, you are worried and troubled about many things. But one thing is needed, and Mary has chosen that good part, which will not be taken from her." Martha was distracted from experiencing Jesus despite the good works that she was doing, and possibly because of them. When you're simply doing, it's easy to reduce God to black and white – to see yourself as right or righteous, and others as "not getting it." Martha truly loved Jesus and wanted to bless Him, and Jesus never criticized her for doing good works. But Martha lost sight of the most important issue – spending time with Jesus.

Mary, on the other hand, just kept going deeper and deeper. She was always at the feet of Jesus [John 11:32, John 12:3]. As Mary contemplated Jesus, I'm convinced there were many shades on the palette, colors … kroma. I'm guilty of being too oriented like Martha. Sometimes, I wish there was a third sister, Marsha, who was the best of both. Then, I could try to be the middle one. But there isn't. I simply need to realize that if I'm going to go deeper, beyond black and white, I need to simply spend more time with Jesus. I choose to go deeper and I hope you will, too.

CHAPTER TWO

LOST AND FOUND

[CAN INNOCENCE LOST BE RESTORED?]

WHAT'S **MISSING?**

Have you ever lost something really important and not even realized that it was missing for a long time? Last Sunday, I heard an announcement telling people that if they've lost their Bibles they are possibly at the lost-and-found located at the welcome center of the church. We hear these announcements about every three to four months. Occasionally, people forget their Bibles at the church, so the ushers gather them to the lost and found, expecting them to be claimed within the week.

Sometimes I'm perplexed by the whole lost and found concept. I wonder how someone can forget their Bible, and not notice, or not care that it's missing. These are often very nice and presumably expensive Bibles. However, their real value would be difficult to measure in dollars and cents. These Bibles are often well worn from years of use; and they're full of "microscopic" precious notes written in the margins. Notes encrypted with revelation from God. Some have a rainbow of highlighter shades. Presumably there is some secret key that reveals the code. For example, green highlighter symbolizes verses that help you grow, and purple represents promises from God, etc. The pages have been inadvertently dog-eared simply by the process of opening and closing so many times that corners were accidentally folded. I love to see Bible pages that have been handled so many times that the oils from the owner's fingers have colored the pages. I wonder how do we lose something presumably important, and not even realize we've lost it?

Losing your dog is not like losing a Bible or an expensive pair of sunglasses. To come home and find a yard gate open and a family pet gone is terrifying. Hearts race and you excitedly call, hoping to see your dog come running from down the street, but he doesn't. Kids and parents begin to frantically search every room, and canvas the immediate neighborhood like a military recon mission. The hours pass, and still no sign; your dog is definitely lost. Signs are posted with a description and photo. A reward is offered, and you wait. Then the animal shelter is surveyed, so many dogs and cats … but *yours* is not there. Children are encouraged that there's still hope, but as the days and weeks pass, hope fades like the last light before sundown. Then there is only dark; hope has disappeared and dreams are shattered. Grief invades like a conquering army, and we are resolved to our new fate our new condition, what we have become.

Losing anything is upsetting. Losing something loved and cherished is gut-wrenching. But, losing hope is overwhelming. The loss of the possibility of restoration compels a person to see their circumstances in a new paradigm. What was lost cannot be restored, so we shall move on and try to make the best of it.

LOSS **OF INNOCENCE**

The first lost-and-found was organized in Paris in 1805. Napoleon ordered his chief of police to establish the office as a central place to collect all objects found in the streets of Paris. Lost and found offices at large organizations handle a large and varied collection of articles. It is reported that transport for London's lost property offices (which handle items lost on the city's Tube, buses and taxis) handles over 130,000 items a year, including 24,000 bags and 10,000 mobile phones; among the more peculiar items that have been handed in include a wedding dress, ashes in an urn, a grandfather clock, a kitchen sink, and several wheelchairs. But, there is one item that has never been returned or claimed at a lost and found.

Innocence is a perplexing thing to lose. The search for the loss of innocence is unparalleled. Sometimes, innocence is lost and we don't even realize that it is missing, like the misplaced Bible. Sometimes, we explore the loss of innocence as a concept. We explore it as an abstract principle that is perhaps close to us, but kept at arm's length. For example, we bemoan that kids are growing up too fast. They're exposed to things on the internet, TV, and movies and they lose their innocence. Even if it's your child, that's still a mere concept.

The concept of the loss of innocence can be explored as an epic quest, and even still remain at arm's length. In 1667, John Milton, long considered the supreme English poet, published *Paradise Lost* in ten volumes [the second edition published in 1674 would comprise twelve books]. Milton was a poet, philosopher, historian, man of political influence, and was readily familiar with theology. Milton revealed that he sought to illuminate the paradox between a sovereign God and man's free will. The context is Adam and Eve's disobedience, rebellion, and fall from grace — the first loss of innocence.

As Milton explores the conflict, he embellishes the biblical account. His story unfolds with Satan's rebellion, along with fellow angels who have been cast out of heaven. The fallen angels devise a scheme to corrupt and destroy God's beloved creation. Satan disguised as a serpent tempts, flatters, and deceives Eve. Eve marvels that an animal can speak, and the serpent replies that it was by eating from the Tree of Knowledge. Eve succumbs to the temptation and is overwhelmed with grief. She frantically searches for Adam.

Adam has been making a flower wreath for Eve, when Eve finds him; he drops the wreath and is horrified. He recognized that Eve ate of the forbidden fruit. Adam chooses to be with Eve, rather than remain pure and lose her. So Adam eats of the fruit as well. Adam and Eve must be punished, and the Son is sent to minister justice and mercy. The curse of sin and death – the children of Satan - are unleashed upon the earth. Adam and Eve become angry and blame one another. The tension mounts and Adam wonders why God ever created Eve. Eve fears Adam's rage, and is terrified that he will leave her. She begs him not to abandon her, and assures him that they can survive by loving each other.

Eve is so upset that she ponders suicide, but Adam intercedes. They agree to enact revenge upon Satan by choosing to remain obedient to God. They pray, God hears their cry, and He sends Michael the archangel to Earth to escort Adam and Eve from Paradise. God reveals a vision to Adam of humankind's future. Adam sees his children and his children's children and the impact of sin and death, lust, greed, envy and pride. The desire for pleasure, and the death and destruction seen in its wake, is exposed. Against this dark background, God reveals His love and plan of redemption for mankind. Adam sees the Son's sacrifice to save man, and then, after this vision, Michael leads Adam and Eve, who slowly and woefully leave Paradise hand in hand into a new world.

I wonder why Milton wrote *Paradise Lost*. What motivated him to pen this epic poem? England had been in a civil war, and Milton sided with the Commonwealth led by Oliver Cromwell. Ultimately, the Royalists were returned to power, and the revolution failed. Perhaps Milton explored his personal despair regarding the failure of the revolution and the nation's loss of innocence. Yet, he affirms optimism in human potential. Was it perhaps an exploration of his personal loss of innocence?

TABOO **WASTELAND**

The personal loss of innocence is rarely explored; it is a taboo wasteland of rotting, lifeless corpses too painful to expose. Pastors, social commentators, and philosophers guard the perimeter, but no one is encouraged to go in and explore. Ironically, mental health professionals invite us in, but don't seem to know the way out.

I was having lunch the other day when I bumped into Carl. He and I go to the same church, and we recognized one another. He starts to share some of his life story with me. He's an engineer, and it sounds like a very capable one. He's attending Bible College and loves to consider deep things of God. He's experienced a personal renaissance in his relationship with God during the last four years.

He shared with me that, "I've been a Christian all my life ... then puberty happened and I fell away for years." I wanted to ask, "What do you mean, 'puberty happened'?" It's not that I'm so naive that I couldn't read between the lines, and it's not that I wanted to be a voyeur. Rather, I wanted him to wrestle with what happened. Yet, I lost the wrestling match in an effort to overcome the guardians of that forbidden question so silent I remained.

It is a shame to lose something precious and not know that it's gone. To never realize something valuable has been forsaken. Ironically, often we don't know that we've lost something until we need it. Typically, when we realize that we have lost something valuable, we search. We retrace our steps in the hope of finding and restoring. Alas, not with innocence. At least that's how it was for me.

When I was 13 years old, innocence was lost. Thirteen is an age when young boys become aware of rites of passage, a time when they become increasingly aware of changes. For some it is as innocent as a Bar Mitzvah, but for others, like me, it was not. Puberty, hormones, selfishness, and a lack of restraint are a dangerous cocktail to mix. This cocktail was destructive like a Molotov.

When virginity is lost, other than in marriage as God intended, there are often adverse consequences. When two lose their purity, the loss is compounded, and emotions are multiplied. One expects there to be feelings of joy and ecstasy, and perhaps there were, but they were short-lived. Instead those feelings were replaced with guilt, shame, and a sense of wrong that led to cold indifference. I then despised her and myself. I'm not even sure today how she felt. I was probably too selfish then to care. I was not religious, but I knew that I was wrong. I knew that I had just unleashed pain, and that things would soon fall apart into meaningless fragments that could not be restored.

When one loses something and has no hope of its restoration, then one resolves to move on, perhaps even trying to fill the void, like the family that gets a new pet to replace the lost one. And so it was for me. I became caught in a vortex with a downward spiral ending in a black hole. Drugs, alcohol, a series of relationships, and other bad choices became my companions. And as I approached the black hole, the gravitational force was so strong I feared that I would be consumed and never find my way out.

When you get to a point where you presume that finding your innocence is impossible, that the size of the reward is immaterial, and that innocence can't be purchased, the only color on your palette is black.

As I look back, from a vantage point many years removed, I ponder the question, "Where was Jesus?" Did I ignore his gentle whispering as He attempted to stop me? Did I not yet recognize the sound of His voice? Did I silently scream for Him to "shut up" so that my conscience was silenced? Did He simply leave me to my own desires as part of His great plan for my life? Why didn't He stop me from myself? This is the same paradox that Milton explored: despite the fact that God is sovereign, I have the ability to make choices and I'm responsible for the consequences. I can lose my innocence, but I also have the opportunity to see it restored.

HOPE **OF RESTORATION**

Why are some people so full of hope of restoration? The other day, I saw a sticky-note on the dining room table that said, "Full deck" and I asked my wife, Karen, "What's this 'full deck' note, do you need this?" She explained that she had been playing a card game with our boys, and all 52 cards were in the deck, so she put the note, "full deck," on the cards. I asked what seemed like a reasonable and logical question, "Why do you need the note?" It was then that she explained that she had other decks of cards in the drawer that were missing cards, so the note, "full deck," distinguished them. This is what I think is remarkable. Most cynical people would simply throw away the decks that were missing cards, but not my wife. She has hope of restoration. She expects that one day the missing pieces will be discovered and things will be made whole. People who have been restored, who appreciate and appropriate restoration, are confident that things that are lost can be found. They are confident that not only cards and missing socks, but more importantly, people will be restored.

Where do you find hope of restoration, the hope that innocence lost can be found? John Milton published *Paradise Regained* in 1671, four years after *Paradise Lost*. Milton used four books to paint a picture of redemption compared to the 12 books that comprised the canvas of his picture of the fall. The latter work was based on the Gospel of Luke's account of the Temptation of Christ. Everything lost in the first epic is regained by the end of *Paradise Regained*. Jesus' perfection is contrast with the shame of Satan.

In *Paradise Lost*, Adam and Eve fall victims to their desire; but in *Paradise Regained*, Jesus resists the temptation, and ultimately reverses the fall of mankind. The moral is that innocence can be found and restored.

The primary message of God's story is the hope of restoration. What man lost in the Garden of Eden, Jesus restored at the cross. Essentially, God desires to forgive us and restore our innocence. Try to imagine for a moment the dilemma. God is completely perfect, and yet He loves people. He wants to spend time with us, just like He spent time with Adam every day before rebellion entered the picture and innocence was lost. Before rebellion, man's relationship with God is like a beautiful picture. Once we lose our innocence we are separated from God. Losing our innocence means all aspects of rebelling against God; it's not really about losing your virginity. Dishonoring God, telling a lie, hating others, selfishness, and taking something that doesn't belong to you are all examples of things presumably all of us have done that are rebellion or sin. It's like an ugly stain has wrecked the picture of our relationship with God.

For example, one morning I was teaching a School of Ministry class at our church. I was using the dry-erase board, filling it up with observations from the class. As I went to erase, I made the discovery that the marker I was writing with was not dry erase [i.e., permanent marker]. The eraser wiped much of the ink, but in essence, it was merely smudged. The board was marred by smeared permanent marker. It seemed that nothing would remove the stain. I used plenty of elbow grease, a host of household cleaners, but nothing could take away the stain. That's how I felt about my shame, guilt, and loss of innocence. That's how I felt about me. My best efforts couldn't restore the original beauty that was lost.

Then one of the students revealed the answer: You simply write over the stain with a dry erase marker, and then erase. Amazingly, the stain was removed! That is how I would describe my experience with Jesus. He came and gave His life so that I could be restored, so that my innocence could be found. What He did for me was something I couldn't do for myself. I knew I was guilty and couldn't make it right, but He could and He did. Jesus provides the opportunity to be restored in my relationship with God, and for innocence lost to be restored. I get to choose to have a relationship with God on His terms or to remain lost.

Now the pictures on the dry-erase board of my life look a lot different than the ones that darkened my life before. I'm excited to see what the future holds. I've learned that dark stains can be erased. By the way, lost dogs do get found; there are happy endings, and there is hope in Christ, for innocence lost will be found.

CHAPTER THREE

TOP DOG

[WAS JESUS A REVOLUTIONARY?]

ESTABLISHMENT **OR ANTI-INSTITUTIONAL**

Have you ever wondered how to keep a relationship fresh? Do you ever consider the conflict between our institutions and the desire to keep a relationship fresh? I'm sitting in a local coffee house drinking a cup of tea; it's a mixture of green and black tea [really just one green, and a black tea bag ... nothing too exotic]. When I came home from Kenya I began drinking more tea. It's a former British colony, and everyone drinks tea. So now I drink tea, but I'm not really a "tea drinker," I'm a coffee drinker, that's why I called the cafe a coffee house, not a tea hut, house or joint [you get the picture]. I love coffee, like some people love pizza — but that's another story.

I've ordered tea, because I'm not thrilled about their coffee. Now I appreciate that this enterprise (on a corporate scale, their revenues probably exceed several developing nations' economies) has done much for the coffee community. They are, dare I say, the "green monster" that cannot be ignored in any contemporary assessment of the state of coffee. Not only do they offer a veritable boatload of coffee but I can also get music and learn a foreign language. I cannot order medium; I'm compelled to order *grande* beverages. Maybe I struggle with my perception of this coffee company as an institution or "the Establishment." I'm sure that's part of the issue, but most likely it's because I don't like their espresso drinks. I was not bemoaning what I perceived as their inadequacies until I began to think about the fact that I've ordered tea.

My drink of choice is a cappuccino. Cappuccino is a coffee-based drink made with espresso, hot milk and foam. A cappuccino differs from a café latte. Lattes are made with twice the amount of milk as a cappuccino, and little to no foam. Cappuccinos are traditionally served in porcelain cups, the better to retain heat as compared to glass or paper. Cappuccinos were created in Vienna's cafes in the 19th Century. The name is derived from the brownish-red color of the Capuchin friar's robes that resembled the beverage.

The cappuccino is the most difficult espresso-based beverage to make properly because of the art - not the science - of making proper foam. As the milk is steamed, air is introduced, and if done properly, it produces a velvety texture and sweetness.

As upscale coffee bars sprang up everywhere in the mid-1990s, cappuccinos became widely available, but not necessarily good ones. When I want a great cappuccino, I'll drive 15 miles to Peet's coffee. To get to Peet's I must drive through Camarillo, through Oxnard, and a good part of Ventura. All this is done in anticipation of a masterpiece, a perfect cappuccino.

Peet's was a pioneer of America's coffee craze. Peet's first coffee house was opened in 1966, just a few blocks from Cal Berkeley. It was an extremely turbulent time in our country and Cal was an epicenter. Peet's attracted plenty of bohemian types, but there was no bohemian agenda, there were just plenty of bohemian types in the nearby area. Today, Peet's is fairly establishment in many ways, but back in the day I imagine it was a great place to enjoy a great cappuccino and observe the struggle between the establishment and those calling for change.

Nearby the original Peet's, is an icon of 1960s Berkeley, opened the same year as Peet's. It is a bohemian expression of haute cuisine, known as "top dog." Top dog is a hole in the wall known for great sausages: knackwurst, bockwurst, kielbasa, bratwurst, linguica, calabrese, hot links and all-beef N.Y. franks. The rolls are soft, but toasted, and there is a variety of mustards. Real sausage aficionados apparently would never disgrace a dog with relish or mayo.

It is not only the sausages served in this hole in the wall, but the walls themselves. They are covered with what this establishment has affectionately referred to as "properganda." Here's a representative sampling that should reveal the flavor: "Any power must be an enemy of mankind which enslaves individuals by terror or by force, whether it arises under the Fascist flag or the Communist flag. All that is valuable in human society depends upon the opportunities for development accorded the individual" [Albert Einstein, 1933]. "Whoever desires liberty, should understand these vital facts: That every man who puts money in the hands of the "government" (so called) puts into its hand a sword which will be used against himself, to extort more money from him, and also to keep him in subjection to its arbitrary will ..."

The walls are filled with quotes and musings that resonate an anti-establishment, near anarchistic, tone that reflects the current culture of this, dare I say, establishment; but also harkens back to an epic era of Berkeley lore. The late 1960s were a time of unrest at many college campuses, but perhaps Cal was most infamous. Battle lines were drawn, Flower Children versus the Establishment. The conflict mirrored the widespread social tensions that tended to flow along generational lines regarding the war in Vietnam, race relations, social mores, and women's rights, traditional modes of authority, experimentation with psychedelic drugs and opposing interpretations of the American Dream. People were calling for change – the status quo was not working for an increasing number of young people. The youth were calling for a new fresh perspective, for a reconsideration of institutions, for renewal of the Establishment. Generations shall always experience conflict as institutions are called into question, and the Establishment is challenged.

The conflict erupted on May 15, 1969, at a place near campus called "People's Park," in an event that would be called "Bloody Thursday." There were almost 6,000 protesters and 800 law enforcement officers from varying jurisdictions. When the battle ended more than 125 protesters and bystanders were hospitalized, countless injured, and James Rector, a student bystander, had died from shotgun wounds.

California Governor Ronald Reagan, sent almost 3,000 National

Guard troops to occupy the city and restore order. The City of Berkeley was occupied for two weeks. The streets were barricaded with barbed wire, freedom of assembly was denied, and a nighttime curfew was imposed. Two weeks later, on May 30, 1969, the city issued a permit allowing people to gather and protest the occupation by the National Guard, and the events of "Bloody Thursday." In a now iconic image, young girls slid flowers down the barrels of bayoneted National Guard rifles.

The same tensions erupted in even more violence and death in the confrontation that occurred less than a year later at Kent State University in Ohio.

Whenever we ignore the need for change and the desire to keep things fresh, there will be death. Not necessarily violence, but nonetheless death — often slow death like rust consuming an unprotected car in a junkyard.

The violence at Berkeley and Kent State compelled America to reexamine its conscience with respect to its treatment of disaffected American youth. The next few years brought an end to the Vietnam War and the birth of a broad array of social change. The events were undoubtedly a catalyst for change. The desire to keep things fresh requires change and change is generally in conflict with the Establishment.

WAS **JESUS A REVOLUTIONARY?**

As I consider the events at Berkeley, I try to consider what would Jesus do? I don't mean in the cliché sense of stopping to help someone with a flat tire, or letting someone else have the last slice of pizza. Rather, I ponder where Jesus might fit in the scenes surrounding the events at Berkeley. Would Jesus take one side or another? Would He heal the wounded?

Would Jesus stop the protests or would He lead them? Would

Jesus place flowers down the muzzles of bayoneted National Guard rifles? Can you see Him in the midst of the chaos? Where is He? Where did you place Him, and what does that say about how you see Him? I wonder, would Jesus be beaten, or possibly shot? Would He be in the governor's office? What would He say or do?

Jesus does not fit conveniently into a neat compartment, just another of the many things I love about Him. He does not seem to me to be an anarchist. Jesus came to fulfill the prophecies and requirements of the Mosaic Law, not abolish them [Matthew 5:17]. Yet, I firmly believe that Jesus is anti-institutional.

Jesus constantly confronted and corrected the religious Establishment. In the Sermon on the Mount he repeatedly declares, "You have heard it said …, but I say to you." I believe that He was trying to help them, and us, discover that we try to approach God simply by trying to follow rules of behavior. Oftentimes, we tend to elevate ourselves by the apparent compliance with these ideals, which in essence is simply spiritual pride. Trying to establish our righteousness through ritual activities or good works simply results in dead religion.

Jesus wants to show us that God loves us and wants to have a relationship with us. The purpose of the Mosaic Law is to show us that we can't measure up to God's standards by our efforts, and therefore Christ came and gave His life to be a bridge between God and man. God will have a relationship with anyone who will approach based on what Jesus has done for them, not their own righteousness. What God desires is relationship, not ritual, religion or institutions.

RELATIONSHIP, **RITUAL AND RELIGION**

The problem seems to be that relationship tends to devolve into institutions, and institutions become ritual, and ritual becomes lifeless orthodoxy known as religion. Fortunately, or unfortunately, depending upon your perspective, '60s types tend to become Establishment types … they become institutionalized. Their desire to rail against "the man" tends to subside, and they become "the man." I'm not sure it's a principle of physics, but I see the relationship like this: we go from emotion, to motion, to slow motion. We then go through the motions – slow, orchestrated, and uninspired.

Yet, slow motion is still motion. There is a spark of life that has not been quenched, that still smolders. I believe that Jesus desires to come and fan the flame so that a fire burns and yearns for intimacy with God, and will not be satisfied with institutions. Anti-institutional types tend to embrace this thought; it resonates with them. On the other hand, what they resent, perhaps most of all, is the notion that they have developed institutional tendencies.

My friend Armando may be an example of this idea. His former passport picture depicts him with long hair and a beard, looking somewhat like Ernesto "Che" Guevara, a potent symbol of rebellion and the zeal of revolution. Armando is presently the executive administrator of our church, after retiring from a successful career in management at Verizon. Gone is the very long hair, but the desire to grow it again remains. That's one of the things, among many, that I love about Armando.

He's a great administrator, and we often remark that nothing falls through the cracks while he's on a project. Yet, despite plenty of years within an established corporate hierarchy, there is a desire for a fresh relationship with God that is not institutional. Also, despite the Che Guevara-esque passport shot, Armando is not a revolutionary. He does not want to blow-up the church to set everyone free to worship God in anarchistic freedom. He understands the church has a role to help people grow in their relationship with Jesus.

My lovely wife is another anti-institutional type. In 1986 she walked from Denver, Colorado, to Washington D.C. as part of the Great Peace March. It was a protest against nuclear arms, and she was inspired to send a message to bring change. Nevertheless, in the last 20-plus years, she has developed some Establishment tendencies. For awhile she drove a white minivan — not her first choice. She would prefer an urban assault vehicle (she tells me they're safe for the kids). We also have our tract home in the suburbs that can help foster some institutional values. Despite these pressures to "conform," she has maintained an anti-institutional approach to Jesus that is not only fresh, but is refreshing. I would be remiss if I neglected to share with you how she played bass guitar on one of the worship teams at church, and wore camo fatigues, and brown bandana on the platform (not the typical pastor's wife uniform).

ANTI-INSTITUTIONAL **RELATIONSHIP**

What does it mean to be anti-institutional in relationship with Jesus? First, what it is not. Anti-institutional is not anarchy, and it is not revolution. Anti-institutional does not seek to rebel against authority simply because it is authority. Suffice it to say that it would be impossible to yield to God if we can't yield to authority.

Anti-institutional would seem to be almost impossible to describe without creating institutions, but there are some characteristics I've observed, that I desire to embrace. Some of these ideas may even help us to discover how to be anti-institutional. First, it is essential that we seek to relate to Jesus more than church. It can be easy to slip into "doing" church, rather than coming together with others to learn of God and relate to Him. Some of the institutions of church help me to discover Jesus, while some obscure Him. Also, my expectations influence the process. I want to come to experience Jesus, rather than experience church.

Secondly, try to avoid putting God in a box that He didn't

create. I don't think God wants us to create a box for Him that He did not instruct us to build. Perhaps, that is why we don't have the Ark of the Covenant; despite the best efforts of Indiana Jones and others to reclaim it. God doesn't want to be in a box. For example, someone might say that contemporary Christian music can't be worship because it is too loud. Nevertheless, the Scriptures, especially the Psalms, show God instructing His people to worship Him with loud instruments. Learn to distinguish the traditions of men or a particular cultural perspective from God's standards, and learn to embrace God's plan. When people say, "That's how we've always done it." chances are it's a tradition of men rather than God's standard. God says to care for widows, orphans, and the poor. There are countless ways to comply that are presumably acceptable to Him. The instruction to care for those in need is God's standard, but some of the ways we do it can become merely our traditions. Then we do the same thing year after year, and it becomes an institution. Cling to God like a rock, but hold traditions loosely like grains of sand that can sift through your fingers.

Third, seek to keep your relationship with God fresh. When the Hebrews were led by God through the wilderness, He provided food from heaven, manna, to feed them daily. Each day the Hebrews would gather fresh manna. If they tried to hoard a supply, it would rot. God wants His people to learn to depend on Him daily, and to discover that God is always fresh. Although God never changes, He is always fresh ... a wonderful paradox about God. We all want progress, but many of us resist change. Be prepared, ready, and willing to slay some of your "sacred cows."

For example, our church used to host an event called, "Jesus Spares." We would rent a neighborhood bowling alley from Friday midnight until two a.m. We would offer free bowling, and bring a band from church to rock the house. Someone would share a brief message about God's love and His desire for a relationship with us. The place would be packed with hundreds of people and most of them had never been inside a church. The event was incredible, but after two years it went by the wayside. Another "sacred cow" sacrificed to remain fresh.

My tendency and perhaps yours too, is to fall into habits that can become ruts, and they can become the Grand Canyon. For example, I love Baskin-Robbins chocolate chip ice cream. Generally, I would tend to order chocolate chip every time. I compel myself to explore other flavors, and by the way, there really are more than 31. It is probably wise to remember the past and have one hand within reach of it, but don't try to hold to the past so tightly that you put a stranglehold on the present and the future. As one hand is within reach of the past, your other hand needs to extend its reach toward the future, and embrace the present. A relationship with God, like any other relationship, is best when there is a sense of past, present, and future. Expect the present and the future to involve change, otherwise there will be no change, and in essence it will look just like "the past."

In the context of our church, I want to be careful to avoid institutionalism. I want to try to avoid doing an event or a ministry simply because it has worked in the past. Instead, we try to discover what God wants to do [or not do]. I'm learning that sometimes we need to do things in different ways, just for the sake of change. For example, we may switch our order of service such that the teaching is at the beginning, and we can respond with extended worship in song. Sometimes, we'll try something different, simply because we think God is in it, and it seems out of the box. For example, having church in a park rather than on campus can keep things fresh.

Most of us tend to be unwilling to consider just how institutionalized our relationship with God has become. We are generally unwilling to consider whether we are simply relating to an institution such as religion or a ritual, or whether we are relating to the person of God. This seems like a perfect time to reflect on our relationship.

I'm sure Jesus wants us to relate to Him, and to the extent that our institutions and traditions help, they are a blessing. However, when we fail to consider the possibility, and probability, that our institutions have become obstacles, it's probably time for a road trip to top dog, but first let's finish that cappuccino.

CHAPTER FOUR

SOUL

[WHERE TO TURN WHEN
LIFE IS OVERWHELMING]

BLOWIN' **IN THE WIND**

Have you ever felt so overwhelmed that you wanted to give up? Where do you turn for help when life is overwhelming? I was staring at a picture from the summer of love – whether it was color or black and white, I don't recall. The image is a young woman. She is not making a peace sign, holding a flower, nor wearing a medallion. Yet, your first impression would likely be "flower-child." She is beautiful in a way that whispers fresh and real. There is nothing plastic, surgical, or airbrushed, nothing that provokes impurity. Her long hair and clean girl-next-door features evoke innocence. If photos could emit scent, this one would certainly smell like a bouquet of exotic patchouli aromas. As you look at her, you sense that she will name her children after one of the seasons, the elements, or a celestial body.

Despite an era associated with turbulent times, the young woman radiates optimism, hope, love, peace, and more. She silently and almost imperceptibly communicates soul. I remember her in the picture, but I cannot see any other element in the composition of the photograph. I don't remember the background, what anyone was wearing, whoever else that was in the picture, or any other information, except the sense of *soul*. Her gaze beckons. Her eyes seem to have the capacity to look past the superficial and gaze into hidden recesses of spirit and soul.

She is seemingly transparent, like a clear pane of glass on a patio door, so clean and clear you might bump into it not even realizing it is there as you venture beyond. Her long hair cascades like spun golden threads. There was no wind on that day to blow her hair. Things were still, and all was calm. But seasons change. The one sure constant about life is change. And change is "blowin' in the wind."

The woman in the picture is my dear friend Elaine. She is often affectionately known as "E." She is not only a wonderful friend, but she is truly dear. She had handed me the picture and was explaining the photo, like when someone shows you images from their vacation, and explains the scenery in the background, when the picture was taken, and who all the people in the picture are. Several summers had passed since the photo was taken. E had experienced seasons of life – marriage, children, and even a grandchild. Yet, the years have been incredibly kind to her countenance. She remains truly lovely. E says that going back to look at an old photo can be refreshing.

You would never think of Elaine as a grandmother. It is true that she makes the best fresh peach cobbler and English toffee in the world. Her toffee is so unbelievably good that at the Christmas party gift exchange people trade every other gift to get the toffee. These qualities do have a maternal nature, but she is so young at heart, no one ever associates her as a grandmother. Some people never grow up because they are simply immature. I've heard that the difference between men and Treasury bills is that, sooner or later, T-bills mature. E is not immature; to the contrary, she has had enough of life – perhaps too much hardship – to forge a mature godly woman. Her youth is not immaturity, but a certain energy that seems to flow directly from God into her, and then from her to others.

E dresses with a style that is young, hip, and contemporary, but remains timeless. Sometimes, I see a man or a woman try to be hip and attempt to dress like "today's generation" and it is a nightmarish caricature that the fashion police would surely censure. But not Elaine; she pulls it off naturally, flawlessly, and effortlessly. They say that certain entertainers [and others] lust to keep a youthful appearance, and would trade their soul with the Devil in exchange for youth. It seems that E found a better way she trusted her soul to Jesus.

Elaine works at our church. She is the administrative assistant, and is often the first person that people encounter when they visit the church office. I'm glad that people see Elaine when they visit the church office because few people reflect Jesus as well as E! People who come to the church office are often hurting or in crisis – like when people go to the doctor, an attorney, or call a plumber. There's often a problem that necessitates intervention. She is so loving and caring that it reminds me of Jesus.

She seems to connect with the very soul of people. She listens tirelessly, genuinely cares, and points them to God. She shows the heart and soul of Jesus: to simply love people. Unfortunately, too often church leaders have an agenda – people are seen as commodities. When people are seen as commodities, or tools, to accomplish a church leader's agenda, it quenches the Spirit of God. The Spirit of God refreshes like a cool breeze. The problem happens when we quench that Spirit. When you encounter E, the presence of God radiates and refreshes like a cool breeze blowin' in the wind.

KATRINA – DISASTERS HAPPEN

When Hurricane Katrina devastated sections of Mississippi and Louisiana, thousands of volunteers came alongside government agencies to assist the relief effort. Elaine and I joined a team of volunteers from our church to provide assistance and share the love of God. We were stationed in the French Quarter of New Orleans, near St. Bernard Parish. The entire parish of St. Bernard was devastated by the 25-foot surge of water that swept through the city destroying everything in its path. The area's 67,000 residents were all displaced; and each of the more than 25,000 homes was declared unlivable. Cars were swept away for blocks as easily as a child would toss Matchbox toy cars across his room. Block after block in every direction, every home was ruined.

One of our assignments was to clean out a home. Eight of us spent two days clearing the home of debris. Everything was removed from the house down to the frame. After two grueling days, I remember looking down the street, and across the block, trying to contemplate the scale of the disaster. At times, it felt like a kid at the beach with a plastic shovel and pail, trying to remove all the sand. There was just too much need. Jesus reminded us, "The poor you have with you always." There will always be needs that require compassion. Life and disasters happen.

Our primary responsibility on the trip was to prepare meals for some of the government agency personnel headquartered at our base. We worked 12- to 16-hour days for eight days, to feed a couple hundred folks three meals a day. Here, once again, Elaine brought the heart and soul of Jesus to those in need. She loves like a mother hen cares for her chicks. Many of the relief workers were exhausted and were fighting the emotional impact of the disaster. There were National Guard troops with their automatic weapons, but they were mostly just boys in grown-up bodies and uniforms. Elaine seemed to care for so many of them. She'd ask where they were from. They often replied with the name of a town without mentioning the state. These were often rural communities with a population of 3,000 people. Basically, almost no one outside of the 3,000 locals had ever heard of the place. Yet E always responded as if she knew exactly where their hometown was. She seemed to serve up compassion and mercy with every scoop of jambalaya or gumbo.

Many of the people of New Orleans had lost all of their possessions, lost their homes, and lost everything that gave them any sense of "normal life." Most of them had no expectation or desire for us to instantly make it all better. What I think most people are looking for at a time like that is to know that someone cares. Elaine sat and listened, seemingly forever, as people shared their story. She brought the heart and soul of Jesus to an area that others described as "Godforsaken." God had not forsaken the people of New Orleans He sent Elaine and others to represent Him.

I'm not sure that you need to experience pain and suffering to
show compassion to others, but people who live in "ivory towers"
are not generally the most empathetic people I know. To feel
another person's pain, we often need to have experienced some
heartache ourselves. That seems to be one of the primary reasons
why Jesus came to our world, so that He could experience our
condition – our pain. Jesus knows that disasters happen, and His
heart has been broken over our condition ... time and time again.
Elaine too had experienced disappointment and heartache –
disasters happen.

WEDDINGS: HOPE — WHERE DREAMS AND REALITY CONVERGE

E is the wedding coordinator at our church. She assists couples
as they plan their wedding at the church and tries to make it a
perfect day for the bride and groom. Elaine has many abilities that
qualify her for this role, but two must be noted: her attention to
detail, and her ability to make people feel at ease. Elaine's weddings
are like a symphony. All of the many instruments are in tune and
work in unison to create harmony. There are countless details at a
wedding, and it seems that many of the brides (and most of their
mothers) want it to be perfect. A wedding has a fairytale quality.
A perfect day ending with, "And they lived happily ever after." What
a boring book that would be! No conflict, no struggle, no tension,
nothing to overcome. As attractive as fairytales might be, they
would not create healthy mature people any more than a diet of
cotton candy would. Life has chapters full of dreams fulfilled,
dreams shattered, dreams replaced, and hope restored - chapters
chockfull of reality.

Weddings are one of the most hopeful experiences imaginable.
The bride walks down the aisle and it is surreal. Time seems to
stand still. She is so lovely that the assembly of guests rise to their
feet as if to give her a standing ovation. The pastor begins to
address the couple and reminds them of God's great love for

marriage, His great love for them, and their responsibilities to God and one another. In essence, the pastor is reminding them of God's view of marriage, and their solemn responsibilities. Before they prepare to repeat their wedding vows, the pastor wants to make sure they *really* want to go ahead with this commitment.

Couples full of hope have confidence that all the problems of the past have been overcome, and all the obstacles of the future shall be scaled, like gentle rolling hills that lead to their fairytale castle. With assurance they commit, before God and man, "To love and to cherish, for richer for poorer, in sickness and in health, for better for worse, till death do us part, or till the Lord Jesus comes." In all likelihood, they've anticipated all the blessings, and assumed they will never have to carry the heavy burdens. Weddings are where dreams and reality converge.

I'm not sure why Elaine makes weddings so special, or how she learned to make them "perfect." Perhaps it is the British influence. Elaine was born into a wealthy British family in Tanzania, East Africa. Thing were done properly. Tea is served in fine porcelain with milk, and table settings are beautiful to behold. Then, she came to America, lived, settled, married and had children of her own. As the years passed, the children grew and became old enough to make their own decisions. The power to choose is both an awesome gift and a great responsibility. Our choices can bring great joy or break someone else's heart. Like when Adam and Eve chose to eat of the forbidden fruit. It doesn't seem that God was angry at them, as much as it seems that His heart was broken. Bad thinking, bad choices, and bad consequences are the steps to a broken heart. Hearts are rarely broken on wedding days; they are full of hope, and then dreams and reality converge.

GOD **IS FAITHFUL**

Life can be overwhelming. I know that I've felt overwhelmed before, and I'm sure you have too. When dreams and reality converge, dreams often fall victim. People will fail, friends and family will disappoint. When it happens, especially repeatedly, there is a flood of emotion that can resemble a 25-foot wall of water sweeping through St. Bernard Parish. Hearts are broken and feelings are tossed around like cars swept away by flood waters. You survey the damage and feel overwhelmed at the scope ... too much damage.

When people you love make bad choices, there are consequences. Not only consequences for their lives, but those choices smash into your life, too. There is the direct impact like when a wall of water crashes down upon your world. For example, when a teenager goes joyriding in their parent's car and ends up smashing it into a parked vehicle (or perhaps something worse). Then, as the surge of water passes, it leaves standing water that destroys a home. The standing water is like the feelings of anger, disappointment, fear, and heartache — so overwhelming. When your loved ones keep making bad choices, and the bad consequences continue to plague you, it's like living in a hurricane-devastated area. Homes in St. Bernard Parish were unlivable. The water damage had destroyed structures. All the drywall was removed, and all the possessions thrown away. All was stripped away, except the foundation and the frame ... the heart and soul.

Each of us has a "dream house." I don't mean a physical home that would be our ideal place to live, but a dream of what we want our life to be. Those dream homes get damaged by real life. People experience the joys and blessings, but also the burdens and broken hearts. Everything shattered, ruined, and stripped away — exposing the heart and soul, foundation and frame. The desire to rebuild, press-on and continue is rebuffed by the fear of being hurt again. There is the sense of being overwhelmed, like a child at the beach with a plastic shovel and pail trying to clear away the sand.

When we sense an impending disaster, such as a fire or hurricane, one of the first things we seek to preserve are photos.

Photos can refresh like a cool breeze. They allow us to reminisce. Nostalgia is like grammar: you find the present tense and the past perfect. Elaine has experienced it all. Each of us can relate to the feeling of being overwhelmed. The specifics of Elaine's story are therefore nonessential. At times she wanted to give up. The circumstances were overwhelming, desperate, and devastating. Yet, she continued and discovered, again and again, that God is faithful.

When you gaze at a picture, you're taken back to another place and another time. As you focus on a particular person in the picture, you tend to ignore the other people in the image. You don't even remember them being in the picture. Sometimes when I look at pictures, I try to imagine where Jesus was in my life at that time. Where was Jesus in the picture? When life is overwhelming I tend to forget that Jesus is in the picture. Jesus came to heal the brokenhearted, and promised that He will never leave us or forsake us. When you trust your soul to Jesus, you can have peace and continue, even when life is overwhelming.

Many of the photos that I like to look at, and that I like to keep near, are pleasant, joyous and refreshing. They are a delight to view and remember. They bring me to a place where dreams are still preserved. As I gaze at those pictures, I often tend to forget to look for Jesus in the midst, as if I didn't need Him at that moment. I tend to forget that He was there.

Perspective is fascinating to consider when you take pictures: the camera angle, framing of the subject, and the lighting. Perspective is equally fascinating when you *look* at photos – what and who do you see? Many of the times of struggle in our lives, the "seasons of disaster," seem to escape being filmed. Ironically, the news media desires to chronicle disasters, while we want to forget, avoid and hide from personal disaster. We don't want to take pictures of those dark times, or we tend to want to later throw them away. How interesting it is to look back at difficult times, and to find Jesus in the picture. There he was standing by us, comforting, caring, and being faithful.

Sometimes, in the midst of overwhelming circumstance, I want to throw in the towel, to run. I'm tempted to "trade my soul," but it seems that Elaine has the better approach, "I trust my soul to Jesus." Sometimes, I don't know how she manages to cope, but she explains it very simply: "God is faithful!"

One of the great lessons that I learn from E, and other friends like her, is that I can trust God no matter what the circumstances. In this chapter of my life, I hope to learn to trust Him more, and hope you do, too.

CHAPTER FIVE

THE DARK CONTINENT

[EXPLORE THE DESIRE FOR COMMUNITY]

THE **SAFARI**

Have you ever wondered whether animals get lonely? Do animals have a desire for community? What about people? If you travel to Africa, especially Kenya (and I truly hope that you do), you must avail yourself of the opportunity for a photo safari. For it may be a once-in-a-lifetime experience, and, as you can imagine, those simply don't arise as often as any of us would like. Safari means journey in Ki Swahili [Swahili], and derives originally from the Arabic safara, meaning travel. The term is used generically to describe any journey or adventure. For example, a simple bus ride from Kenya to Uganda is a safari. However, the term safari to a European or North American tourist has a different association, big game!

My first experience with safari was at Lake Nakuru game refuge in Kenya, a half-day journey from Nairobi. As you travel along the Great Rift Valley from Nairobi, you ascend to over 7,000 feet above sea level before entering the plains. The landscape is filled with groves of golden acacia trees, small farms, and villages that dot the landscape. The view from the top of the ridge hints at the immensity of the valley, as well as the contrasts of Africa. Africa is a place of contrast: rich and poor, healthy and dying, light and dark. From the apex you see the contrast between arid and fertile. One side of the valley receives minimal rainfall, and the dry soil barely yields sufficient food to sustain life; and the other side displays rich soil in deep brown and red hues providing hope for more — more of life.

As we approached the game reserve we could see Lake Nakuru as we descended from a hill. It was late afternoon, a time when the sky has a golden quality. It's a favorite time for photographers, cinematographers, poets, romantics, and perhaps even some who write in journals — but that's another story. The lake appeared to have a pink tone reflecting from the shore, a presumed optical illusion created by the setting sun. As we entered the park and approached the lake, the reality of the illusion was revealed. The pink hue was created by the presence of tens of thousands of pink flamingos. No zoo or Miami postcard could begin to convey the richness of the image of *these* pink flamingos. There were so many flamingos that the color of the lake, and later the sky, was seemingly transformed by the presence of the enormous flock.

Near the flock were two eyes barely visible above the water line. Soon the massive head and the enormous body of a single hippo would ascend from the water to be revealed in all its massive glory at the shoreline. Hippopotamus is a Greek word meaning *river horse*, but the immensity of this hippo would dwarf any horse that I have ever seen. Its hinged jaw seemingly opens 180 degrees to present a cavern. The contrasts between hippos and flamingos are so many and so obvious that I would be remiss if I wasted precious ink to explore them with you. Yet, there was one contrast that stood out to me that seemed less obvious, and perhaps even worthy of mention: there were thousands of flamingos and one solitary hippo.

One of the spectacular experiences on a photo safari is the presence of enormous herds. Hundreds upon hundreds of gazelle, impala, and cape buffalo walk, run, spring, and thunder across the plain. There are also smaller herds and gatherings of other animals. The giraffes raise above small acacia trees that hide their camouflaged bodies. They prefer the gentle limbs that bear not only leaves, but thorns that extend for more than an inch from the branch. I thought to myself how cool it is that God would create a giraffe with the capacity to use its tongue to carefully pull the leaves from the limbs without being pierced by the thorns. What I saw was more amazing, the giraffes simply swallow the leaves and thorns together with no apparent hesitancy or adverse consequence.

The monkeys and baboons gather in large troops with an apparent social order and hierarchy. Predators take caution before engaging these primates for they can be surprisingly dangerous. They are obviously extremely playful, but one must respect them. Even the predators, such as lions and hyenas, travel in groups with a sense of community. Lions are romantic to consider, and tend to impress for a host of reasons. Hyenas, on the other hand, seem to have horrible public relations and are held in disdain. Both lions and hyenas hunt, live, and survive as a group.

The zebras roam and graze the tall grass in herds. Their stripes not only camouflage them, but remind us once again of the contrasts, the contrasts of Africa, and of life. Then there are the rhinos, both rare black and white rhinos. They are as impressive as a living tank can be. One approaches with caution as these armor-plated, horned, potential living battering rams command respect. Yet, they did not seem aggressive. They were seen occasionally throughout the day as we explored the enormous game refuge.

Then we saw a leopard, the most beautiful of the big cats in my humble opinion, lying across a tree limb only 20 feet away. The leopard was essentially solitary and isolated, so different from the great herds. Despite the sense of awe and reverence at their impressive bodies, I found myself pondering their psyche. I wanted to explore the heart, mind and soul of the leopard.

DO ANIMALS GET LONELY?

Do animals like leopards and hippos get lonely? Do they feel isolated in their apparent lack of community? Did God design them to live in community or is their apparent solitary life a perfect fit? I couldn't help asking the same questions about man.

Africa has been called *The Dark Continent,* a romantic name for an unknown and under-explored region of the world to the Europeans of the 19th Century. Today it is different, and yet, perhaps the same. While Africa has been explored and mapped out, there are still plenty of elusive and uncharted areas of the human experience to explore: to journey, adventure, to *safari* to hidden recesses of the heart, mind and soul.

The slums of Nairobi are densely populated. As my friends and I walked through the streets, we saw tens of thousands of people. Children called out *mzungo* a Swahili word meaning *white man*. In a span of two hours, we had seen thirty to fifty thousand people, but the five of us were the *only* Caucasians – we were a mere novelty. We stood out for all to see, like a bad dress at the Oscars. The *darkness* of the continent had nothing to do with skin color, or exploring geography. The darkness was the feeling of being an outsider who wanted to connect.

It seems that God created man to generally thrive best in community. God looked upon His creation and declared it was very good; and then he helped man realize that it is *not* good for man to be alone. So God allowed Adam the opportunity to see all the animals that He had created, in essence the first safari. Adam realized that he could not have an ideal relationship with any of the other animals, that man was somehow unique. Therefore, Adam needed a companion that would be similar to him, yet different. The companion would be complimentary to Adam so that together they could grow in their relationship with God and one another. Together they would be better protected from danger.

It is interesting to consider that the next chapter in God's story, the third chapter of Genesis, reveals some of the danger of isolation. There, in the Garden of Eden, Eve is alone, separated from Adam, and the Tempter comes. The evil one, the enemy of men's souls, seeks an opportune time to tempt, a time when we are alone and vulnerable. His temptation is always designed ultimately to destroy our community with God, and thereby our community with others. There in the Garden of Eden, perfect intimacy between God and man and between mankind is lost. Perfect light is veiled, shadows and darkness dangerous darkness enter the Garden and the human experience.

The desire for community appears to be part of our DNA. It is not limited to a desire for marriage or physical intimacy, but transcends those plains like the road to Lake Nakuru that reaches a summit that allows us an opportunity to consider the Great Rift Valley below. The panorama spreads out below and travels seemingly forever to the horizon. The horizon is a place where heaven and earth seem to meet. On one side of the valley is an arid, barren, lifeless wasteland — darkness. On the other, is a fertile, fruitful, future and hope, full of life and light. Here, isolation and are community contrasted and metaphorically displayed.

Some seem to be content to be isolated and alone. Perhaps it is a special cloth that God has cut them from. They may be most at peace when they have plenty of space and plenty of time alone to meditate and contemplate. Perchance they have considered that others simply would not understand the depth of their thoughts and feelings, and it is best for them to journey alone, to safari life like a lone adventurer.

DESIRE **FOR COMMUNITY**

For many, perhaps most, there is a desire for community and frustration in the quest for it. They have sought authentic relationship only to feel rebuffed, ignored, and forsaken. They have been cast out into darkness, compelled to conclude that dogs and cats make better friends than people. The darkness of loneliness and isolation is ironically brightened by another species. Then they become resolved to remain on the outside.

What does it feel like to be isolated when you want to connect? The feelings are ethereal like the shadows cast by the setting sun ... long shadows that begin to eliminate the light, shadows that create darkness. The darkness seems to usher in feelings of depression and an enhanced desire to withdraw.

Those feelings fuel further isolation, and beckon us deeper into the cave where light becomes dim and faint. The cave is a place where many journey but, even though many safari there, each one seems to be a place of solitary confinement. No other voices are heard except the voices in our heads, echoing and reverberating off the walls of the cave. Confused, sad, hurt, angry and yearning voices can all be heard.

In the midst of darkness, one is drawn to light. One may be apprehensive, afraid and unwilling to come to the light, but nevertheless the light attracts. One of the cruelest ironies is the fact that many people perceive the church to be one of the darkest places. They are drawn to the church, because of a desire for community and authentic relationship. This is what God has always intended His church to be: the light of the world, and a city on a hill that cannot be hidden [Matthew 5:14]. Intuitively, people are drawn, like moths to a light, expecting to find connection. Yet, the church can so grossly misrepresent Jesus in this area. We obscure His light, and cast shadows.

I was visiting a church recently, a place where I presumably knew no one, and was unknown to them – anonymous, and alone. There were about 500 adults gathered for the service. I had arrived 20 minutes before the service and remained 15 minutes after. Throughout the time that I was there, not a single person offered a greeting, except a "hello" from the "professional greeter" at the entrance to the foyer.

I was reflecting on this experience and how typical it might be. I was wondering how frequently people experience this phenomenon at places of worship. I imagine people passing in parking lots, courtyards and foyers, and silence or the cliché inquiry, "How ya doing?" People asking, and then continuing to walk past, and never stopping to hear the reply, because, they never cared despite the question. I imagine worse still, the question, "How ya doing?" and a person fully opening up and responding "Suicidal."

Then the first person, who never paid attention to the reply in the first place, responds, "Hey, that's great! Good to see ya!" and keeps on walking. Darkness. No light brought in by the question, no light of compassion to bring hope, no light of community, only darkness. How far-fetched does the picture seem?

We are reluctant to explore this issue – the desire for community, the responsibility to provide, and the inability to find it. Many might be willing to journey to the edge of this Dark Continent and consider the social, spiritual, and psychological issues of community as an intellectual issue preferring to keep them at arm's length. However, there seem to be only a few who want to safari there on a personal level, to journey to the heart and soul.

ENGAGING **AND CHANGING**

God seems to be into community. God created man so that He could have relationship with us; and His great desire is for us to be in unity with one another [John 17]. We cannot be in true unity without *community*. God's ideal seems to be that we "one another." The expression is used repeatedly throughout the Bible, and expresses the community experience of real relationships. Here is a sampling of how God wants us to "one another": love, greet, honor, build-up, receive, correct, care for, comfort, consider, forgive, serve, bear with, be kind to, submit to, don't lie to, don't judge, don't deprive, etc.

The early church seems to be God's ideal map for community. People loved one another, shared with one another, grew spiritually with one another as they prayed, studied, and learned about God with one another. They ate with one another, spent time with one another, and generally "one anothered." The early church was a community; not Communism, but a community. Communism, as a philosophy, may be noble, but as a form of government it requires compelling people to share resources with one another, and thus in its very core is distinguished from God's ideal community. God's community is a *voluntary* assembly of "one anothers." The presence of people "one anothering," presumably with God in the very midst, has to be the brightest light imaginable. It is the desired destination for those who safari.

Before we can leave the Dark Continent we must explore the community's responsibility to be inclusive. I think it would benefit the dialogue immensely to realize that although the local church is an institution, and there is generally some organizational frame-work, the *church* is simply a community of people. This safari requires us to consider our individual responsibility; it is essential, since people's lives are affected. Although I do not suggest that I have all the answers, there are a few things that ring true for me. The rest should be spirited thought provoking dialogue that results in action.

First, I have come to realize that arriving at a place where God's people have gathered, and people seem too interested in themselves to extend love, or at least a simple greeting to someone they don't yet know, does not represent God's community to me. Second, "professional greeters" can really turn me off, unless there is a sense of real community. For example, if there is an annoyingly cheerful greeter person who hands me a bulletin, and the rest of the folks don't interact with me at all, then the "professional greeter" simply stands out like a freak in the midst of the sea of lifeless, alien, soulless, mutants "playing church." Interestingly, for me, if "everybody" is annoyingly cheerful, friendly, or engaging, I'm actually attracted. That's the kind of freak show [at the risk of appearing cliché – a "Jesus Freak" show] that I not only want to see, but would tend to want to be part of. I'm not suggesting that "everybody" should approach the same individual and shower the poor soul with attention. What I'm suggesting is that the "poor soul" is observing the so-called community that is "doing church." She either sees people genuinely engaging others, including those who are alone or on the fringe of the community, in other words, being the church; or she sees people who don't engage others, in other words, *playing* church.

The tendency of organizations is to institutionalize roles such that a function or task is perceived as the responsibility of some member of the organization. When the church operates like an organization, rather than a community, the tendency is to "delegate" the function of engaging others to the institution, rather than perceiving the process as an individual responsibility of all members of the community.

I watched this scene unfold just the other day. Fifty people gathered for lunch, a group that seemingly represents a community. Individuals gathered at the buffet line, filled their plates, and sat at round tables. Round tables have tremendous potential for community. There were ten round tables that could each seat eight – plenty of seating. One of the first in line sat down at a table, and waited for others to join. He patiently waited as all 50 got their food and were seated. When the group was seated, there he sat alone.

The irony was that the group that had gathered was comprised of church leaders. Was it merely a group or was there true community? Is it any wonder that people go to bars to find community? If it truly was a community then who was responsible for including the one who sat alone? Where were the empathy and the compassion of Jesus?

There, in the midst of a gathering that in many respects truly represented the light of the world, a shadow of darkness prevailed. The dark feelings of a person, who sat isolated, and undoubtedly wanted community, and the dark reality that God's people were insensitive to the condition. In contemplating the situation, it is too easy to shift responsibility. It is easy to say the individual should have joined others at another table; or to say that *someone else* should have gone over to that one who sat alone.

The darkest thought is to realize that this scene is played out every week at schools, neighborhoods, the workplace, and unfortunately, the church. The Dark Continent is a call to safari, to truly explore the deep, and dark, question, "Where's my responsibility?" What am I actually doing to engage people into relationship – into community? We all need to balance our need to be alone and have some space, and our responsibility to create community. We will not be the light of the world until we confront the darkness.

Finally, people are probably not called to live a seemingly isolated life like a leopard, but we're probably more like the flamingos – together coloring the world around us, and changing the horizon.

CHAPTER SIX

NAVIGATION

[A BETTER SENSE OF DIRECTION]

WHERE AM I GOING?

Do you ever wish that you had a better sense of direction? San Francisco is a great tourist town. It has great restaurants and attractions, fantastic architecture, cosmopolitan senses, and pervasive charm. One year we were enjoying a family vacation in San Francisco when I took the family on an inadvertent sightseeing tour. We had just finished eating seafood at Fisherman's Wharf, and when we were through walking around the shops, we decided it was time to hop in the car and get back to the hotel. That's when the "fun" began.

I made a left turn and soon we were seeing all sorts of famous landmark locations: Ghirardelli Square, Pier 39, the Ferry Building, cable cars, Coit Tower, the Golden Gate Bridge, Chinatown, Little Italy, and finally, we got to our hotel. All the while, my lovely bride was inquiring with varying tones of urgency, "Honey, why don't you stop and ask for directions?" In hindsight it seems like a perfectly reasonable question, but at the time I was wondering why I didn't own a Miata, or another two-seat roadster, so that she couldn't backseat drive. I never stopped for directions, nor did I ever ponder the question as to why I wouldn't stop. Instead, I urged my wife and sons to enjoy the sightseeing tour, and reminded them that people pay good money for these tours.

The next morning, I made the most embarrassing discovery. The discovery was made more painful simply by the fact that my wife made the discovery with me. Our hotel was only one right turn away from where I started my adventure. In other words, if I had just made *one right turn*, I would have turned right to the hotel.

It's too easy to get lost. Perhaps it's a genetic predisposition ... my people wandered in the wilderness for 40 years (apparently, Moses wouldn't ask for directions either). Getting lost is generally not cool, unless it's a divine appointment, but that's another story. Not only is it "uncool," but there are also adverse consequences. I remember when I was 17 I took a date to a concert at a big arena. She was smart, hip, and beautiful. Although the concert was great, and you'd be jealous if I told you the artist (so I'll spare you), I was just focused on her. I was so focused on her, that I paid no attention to where I parked my car. We walked around that huge circular arena parking lot, seemingly for a dozen laps and many miles, before almost 17,000 people left and I found my car. She was not impressed, and as you might imagine, there were adverse consequences.

Sometimes, I wish I had a GPS receiver. The Global Positioning System [GPS] has numerous satellites that orbit the earth and transmit precise signals that allow a GPS receiver to determine its location, speed, direction and calculate time to a destination. The system was developed by the United States Department of Defense. The annual maintenance cost of the system is $750 million. Although the U.S. Government incurs this significant cost, they make the system free for public use. Maybe if I bought a GPS receiver, I wouldn't get lost.

I never felt totally comfortable with a compass. I can't figure out a compass or a map, although I'm sure that they're actually relatively easy to use. When I print directions from some website like MapQuest, I almost always disregard the map and focus on the printed directions. I like to see every turn: where I am, where I want to be, and how long it should take to get there. It would just be easier if I was one of those people who never gets lost.

MORAL **COMPASS**

I imagine my friends Lynn and Valeri never get lost. Lynn is hip and cool and lovely. There are so many things that I love about Lynn. She and her husband Roger (Roger is always limited to simply being Lynn's husband) are some of our best friends in the whole world. She is an artist and she is creative and that in and of itself is a good thing. She loves kids, and would probably be one of those people who would start an orphanage, or become a children's ministry director of a big church where she could mentor hundreds of people to love and care for kids like Jesus does.

Lynn is one of those pseudo-vegetarian types who prefers the salad bar to steaks. I like to ask her whether vegetarians can eat animal cookies, because those are the kind of moral issues that seem appropriate for my level of thinking. Lynn doesn't even bite at the ridiculous bait; she's too deep. Lynn presumably would never eat veal. When Lynn answers questions they are always A+ answers.

Although there are so many admirable qualities, one of my favorites is her sense of direction. Lynn is a conscience among our friends. What makes Lynn cry should make us cry; and what makes Lynn rejoice should make us rejoice. I love to share my stories with her, sometimes just to wait for her reaction. Lynn is a good litmus test for whether something is real, does it penetrate, is there something of value, and is it intrinsically good.

Valeri is another amazing person in my life. She is one of those people who "has it together" but is extremely humble. Her humility is so refreshing to me, like the aroma of strong coffee brewing when I'm up before the sun. Val has her ducks in a row, and could probably herd cats, too. Her vocational pedigree is impressive. She was the administrative assistant for the CEO of one of the world's largest utilities, she worked in the planning department of three cities, and helped to coordinate development for a large real-estate developer. She runs marathons and presumably leaps tall buildings in a single bound. She is an extremely gifted and capable administrator.

There are so many things that I dig about her. She handles pressure situations well and doesn't seem to get upset or ruffled in the midst of intense circumstances. Some people who are task-oriented don't care about people, and I've only met a few who could get a lot done and still find time to genuinely care about others. Val is definitely one of those people.

Val used to work in the office of another church, before we started going to the same church. She ultimately left that job. When she told me her story, I felt like I had encountered Dorothy after she returned to Kansas from Oz. She had ventured "behind the curtain" and was disillusioned by what she saw. One of the most encouraging comments I have ever heard someone share about the church we attend was when Valeri said, "My faith has been restored in the church." It's good to know that God is still alive, and there's hope of meeting Him at church.

One of the things that impressed me most about my friend Valeri is her sense of morality. She has a clear sense of direction about what is right and what is wrong. She doesn't compromise on what is right. I don't mean to suggest that she doesn't compromise when there are disagreements about issues, or that she is self-righteous. Rather, she will not compromise about things that should not be compromised.

For example, I can't imagine Valeri or Lynn lying. They just won't compromise their integrity, their sense of right and wrong, and the truth. I imagine that probably more than anything else, they hate being lied to. I guess most of us don't like being lied to. Some of us are offended by the breach of trust and the betrayal. Some folks, like Lynn and Valeri, apparently see the moral failure and its consequences.

IS THERE TRUTH?

If there are lies, then presumably there is truth. This is a great philosophical issue that probably transcends the relatively mundane issues such as the value of sunscreen, recycling, and whether vegetarians can eat animal cookies. Is there truth?

Moral relativism as a philosophy rejects objective or universal truth. Relativism denies a universal standard for moral absolutes, and embraces the notion that truth is relative to social, cultural, historic, or personal circumstances. Thus, morals become simply a part of cultural boundaries or personal preference. Often, the concept is used culturally to refer to accepting other people's values, and to assert tolerance, but the cultural use is distinct from the philosophical issue.

The case for truth cannot simply be made from the argument of adverse consequences. For example, one might assert that moral relativism tends to generate immorality. It is easy to create an impressive case outlining a host of disturbing social conditions, but something can only be immoral if there is morality. Furthermore, there have also been a host of abuses, or adverse consequences, perpetrated by those who hold the position of absolute truth.

Some might argue that moral relativism tends to be self-justifying. The self-justifying tendency is obvious; however, one does not have to dig too deep to see the tendency for self-justification related to the absolute truth position either. Self-righteousness can flow from both camps, and I dare assert that the discharge can be equally toxic. Moral absolutists and relativists tend to elevate themselves, perhaps equally. The relativists cry the mantra of "tolerance" and want to embrace tolerance of all views, but they are extremely intolerant of the view of moral absolutes. Both sides tend to be intolerant of the other.

Unfortunately, the arguments frequently devolve, and we remain perplexed. What is right and what is wrong? Where are we and where are we going? It is easy to get lost without a sense of bearings to navigate our course. Navigation tends only to be effective if the reference points are reliable and discernible (i.e., visible).

One of the most acclaimed tales of navigation relates to Ernest Shackleton's Antarctica expedition and the voyage of the *Endurance*.

Schackleton is renowned for his leadership skills that preserved the lives of his crew after their ship was destroyed en route to the polar cap. It is a tale of trials, tragedy, and triumph that could rival the great Greek epic poems.

In the Spring of 1916, Shackleton realized that the only chance for survival would be for he and a few of his men to leave Antarctica's Elephantine Island and attempt to reach the small but inhabited island of South Georgia to summon help. On April 24, 1916, Shackleton and five others, including ship captain, Frank Worsley, set out on an 800 mile voyage through some of the world's most extreme oceans. They set sail in a 22-foot boat, the *James Caird*, loaded with rocks for ballast and meager supplies. They sailed for 17 days through storms, and even a hurricane, before they successfully landed on South Georgia Island.

The mere fact of their survival, in light of intense storms and hostile seas, is amazing. Perhaps the most amazing aspect of the voyage was the remarkable navigation of Worsley. He could not rely upon GPS to navigate, and instead used a sextant and celestial navigation. A sextant is a navigational tool that is used to determine the longitude and latitude at sea by measuring angular distances, especially the altitudes of sun, moon, and stars. South Georgia Island is relatively very tiny, set in the midst of immense open and dangerous sea. Slight miscalculations would result in the voyagers missing their destination and meeting certain death. The foul weather allowed Worsley four sightings during the voyage, and those occurred while the boat was tossed on stormy seas. The voyage is heralded as one of the greatest accomplishments of navigation and seamanship ever.

Sometimes, when I consider moral relativism, I feel like I am the navigator trying to find South Georgia Island and arrive safely at a desired destination, all the while periling great adversity. Without the ability to obtain a reading of a known reliable navigation point, it is extremely difficult to know where I am, where I'm going, or how to get to a desired destination.

The desire for a moral compass a conscience of right and wrong, is so attractive to me. I was attending a seminar recently and one of the classes was in ethics. One of the people I was attending with wanted to skip the class, but asked me to grab a completion slip for him, so that he could take credit for being there — at the *ethics* class. The irony would be purely comical if I wasn't compelled to consider the ramifications on a greater scale.

Trust flows from truth, and I want to trust. I don't like to be lied to. I may not be as virtuous as my friends Valeri and Lynn, but it bugs me, too. I don't like being lied to by politicians, salesmen, pastors, friends, etc. I don't like that our culture has devolved into one where lies are expected, accepted, condoned or approved of. I find repugnant the whole notion of color-coded lies. For example, we have white lies, black lies, and, presumably, charcoal grey, and brown lies too.

If two philosophies or belief systems are in conflict, they both can't be true. Either they are both false, or certainly one is false. In moral relativism, everyone is doing what is right in their own eyes, and it seems to me that can't be right. It appears that moral relativism is only likely to aggravate my propensity for getting lost. Not lost in the sense of my driving directions, but lost in the sense of the great moral and spiritual issues of life.

The simple fact that I yearn for truth makes me cling to the hope that there is objective truth. I desire to discover (universal) right and wrong. I want to know that I'm heading in the right direction, and if I've gone off course, to be able to navigate clearly to a desired destination. This desire, one that I hope you share, makes me convinced that truth exists!

RELIABLE **NAVIGATION SYSTEM**

Where do we find truth? Where do we find a reliable navigation system? Perhaps it is because I'm motivated by my recognized propensity to get lost that I've been doing a lot of research into navigation systems. I found one that appears to be reliable, has been tested and approved by many, is not technology dependent, and utilizes a classic design.

As you've probably imagined by now, it's a GPS [God's Positioning System]. Forgive me, because I'm not always as tech savvy as I'd like to be, but I'll try to explain how this thing works as best as I understand it.

Jesus said, "I am the way, the truth, and the life. No one comes to the Father except through Me" [John14:6]. Jesus is the essence of truth. All necessary truth regarding God is manifest in Jesus and is accurately represented in the Bible. God has incurred the cost, and maintains this incredible system to reveal truth so that I can navigate life. Similar to the Global Positioning System established and maintained by the U.S. Government, I simply need a receiver to utilize the system. Jesus explained that He would send the Spirit of truth to guide us into all truth [John 16:13]. The Holy Spirit is the receiver that allows us to use God's navigation system.

Here is one of the really interesting features that distinguish this system. This system, like all the others on the market, tells you where and when to turn to get you to a desired destination. However, for most systems the ultimate purpose is to direct you on a desired course. In other words, the destination is the "bottom-line." God's system emphasizes the journey with Him, not the destination (although the manufacturer offers great assurance and incentives regarding the destination). As you experience the journey it may not always be the shortest distance between two points, but you will safely get to the desired destination.

After researching all the various belief systems and philosophies, I came to realize that this was simply the most effective and reliable navigation system available. It also seems evident that Lynn and Valeri have been using this system with great success. The problem was I had to humble myself to get directions. That's when I learned that I was just one right turn away. Maybe you're closer than you think.

CHAPTER SEVEN

ANOTHER
FOUNTAIN PEN

[WHERE CAN WE FIND
TRUE CONTENTMENT?]

OBJECT **OF MY DESIRE**

Have you ever thought that something or someone could bring you happiness? Before you, or anyone else, read these words in print, they were written in brown ink. I mean the kind of ink that comes in a bottle, not a thin plastic cartridge, although at times I can be fond of cartridges. Cartridges can be like pixy stix, full of fun stuff that is sweet to the palate, but difficult to find in brown.

The words were written with my new fountain pen, another fountain pen, but not "just another fountain pen." This one has been heralded (by others before me, I simply agree) as arguably the most art deco design of any fountain pen ever made. The streamline shape is inspired by the time when the speed of locomotives and airplanes was a novelty. The clip seems to have steps, and there are nine proportional silver bands, hallmarks of the 1920s and 1930s deco period.

These stylistic innovations were reflected in buildings, paintings, furnishings, and appliances of this golden era. The black-resin and ivory-marbled barrel are a beautiful contrast like Shamu, but again that's another story. The nib is etched in fine detailed deco patterns, and is stamped with the numbers 4810. These numbers, at first blush, would seem to represent a serial or model number, but it is the height of the tallest peak in the Alps, Mont Blanc, described in meters. The pen pays homage to art deco, a classic and distinctively American style, and the era in which F. Scott Fitzgerald wrote *The Great Gatsby.*

Pens like this are not a dime a dozen, and come with a price; a euphemism for people who don't want to appear gauche, but want you to understand this is not like the stick-pen that they buy at your office by the boatload for pennies apiece. By now, your curiosity may be piqued about the price of this pen, but mere dollars and cents could not truly tell the tale. For more than dollars and cents, this pen came with a price tag that could only be bartered in exchange for anguish of soul.

It all started with the Pelikan San Francisco. The Pelikan is a fine German fountain pen, one of the oldest and one of the best. Pelikan's precision German engineering brought innovations to the fountain pen filling system, a major evolution to the fountain pens' development. Pelikan produced a series of pens to commemorate famous cities, and thus the San Francisco pen was birthed with brown and green hues. The resin of the cap and barrel, with gold accents, is beautiful to behold.

Alas, the pen did not motivate me. I could no more write with it than I could kiss another woman. I imagine musicians, who hold a beautiful instrument, want to make inspiring music, but if the instrument is not right for them, then there is silence. And the silence is deafening. You develop disdain for the instrument, or for the pen, for it is beautiful but will not excite. It is like the beautiful woman, her shape seemingly defying the laws of physics, like Barbie. But, like Barbie she has no soul. She is plastic, superficial, and cold, pleasing to the eye, but, like fake fire logs, unable to produce warmth, and unable to kindle a fire of soul that exhilarates.

The San Francisco had become a collectible in the marketplace, but to me it was shelved, like a young man's baseball glove when too many Springs have sprung. It gathered dust, only occasionally making a cameo appearance to write something nondescript and functional like a checkbook ledger entry. If others perceived it as valuable, then I could trade it for something I really wanted … something that would inspire, something that could satisfy. And thus the plot was conceived.

THE **PLOT**

Unfortunately, a pen with a price tag cannot be simply acquired for a San Francisco. The pot had to be sweetened. What else could I add to the deal to make it happen? I looked at my pseudo-collection of pens for appropriate bait to make the deal happen. I felt like a general manager of a major league baseball team, desiring to make a trade to acquire that mystical player who could finally make the team a contender. Like Brando in *On the Waterfront*, desiring to be a contender can come with a price tag paid from the soul. I surveyed my roster and there were two players on the team who were definitely *not* going to be traded.

First, the Delta Israel, a beautiful pen created to commemorate the 50th Anniversary of the Nation of Israel. In 1998, they made 1,948 of these fountain pens. Blue lapis and white marbled ivory resin symbolize the colors of the flag of Israel. The pen has a silver band adorned with Stars of David and is etched with a number to confirm that it's part of an exclusive club, part of this limited edition.

The other, the Coliseum, another limited edition, was also off-limits. Designed and inspired to commemorate an anniversary of Rome's most famous monument, the barrel is hewn from orange resin, with black contrasting cap, not the contrast of cheap Halloween decorations, but the tasteful elegance of a work of art. Its silver band is etched with the laurel wreath, symbolic of the crown that was bestowed upon the champions in the competitions that made this monument famous. The pen has a lever filler system, a design introduced in the deco era, but with imperfections. Now it was reintroduced as a conquering hero, harkening back to another era, to a golden era.

Both of these pens would *not* be traded. They had been presents from my wife (although I selected them, and requested them, it just seems best to rationalize that they were from her). They were both earmarked for my two sons, currently they are too young to fully embrace the subtle nuances and beauty of these treasures. One day I hope they would embrace these pens and treasure them as their father had; and each time they wrote with them they would be inspired, as if some divine energy was coursing through their veins, through the reservoir of ink, and through the beautiful nibs of precious metal to paper. Paper eager and waiting to capture their precious ideas like a person scurrying around a smooth wooden floor to pick-up pearls that had cascaded from a broken necklace. And, Lord willing, they would fondly reflect upon their father and the legacy of fountain pens, perhaps the only material inheritance they would receive.

I looked again at the roster of players on my pen team. There were not many prospects of value. It was not really a true collection in any proper sense of the term ... but there were two pens that could sweeten the pot, and could possibly make the deal happen. Would I be willing to trade them?

A general manager rarely has to negotiate the personal issue of sentimental involvement with a player. Certainly, he must consider the fans' sentimental connection, because that generates revenue, and alas isn't it all about the bottom-line? Generally, the issue isn't sentiment, but whether I am trading too much away for what I'm receiving, and did I get something in return that makes me better ... a contender?

These two pens that I was considering trading raised the simultaneously beautiful and hideous faces of sentimental connection. First, there is a beauty in being able to connect an inanimate object, such as a pen, to people and events and to form bonds. Then, there is a grotesque and hideous face of being willing to sever those bonds for another possession ... to sell-out. Both stared at me in the mirror, but I quickly looked away before sentiment and emotional attachment could pierce my heart.

One of the pens was a Meisterstuck (masterpiece) 149, the largest of the standard-issue pens Montblanc makes. It seems to be the size of a souvenir baseball bat. A dear friend gave it to me, because he couldn't stand fountain pens, and he knew that I loved them. He, dear soul that he is, simply wanted to bless me.

The other was a Waterman opera, black with a herringbone pattern, a reminder of a golden era in so many ways. Again, it was a gift from my wife. True, I had picked it out, and requested it, but I made sure she pulled the trigger (one cannot be too careful you know). That, in and of itself, should have stopped me, but it's worse: the pen was presented to me on our first anniversary. This pen, unfortunately, had mechanical problems that in effect made it unusable to me, but in the capable hands of a pen smith, could presumably be restored and would likely sweeten the pot enough, even in its current condition, to make the deal I wanted to happen.

I wrestled, suspended between the points of my predicament, but the wrestling match did not last long enough and my new pen would reign victorious. It would vanquish sentiment, and prevail, or so it seemed. What could make a man do such a thing? Surely, it was not a capital offense. Yet, I had traded virtuous affection, sentiment, and emotional treasure for something, for some "thing," albeit a glorious deco masterpiece. What would compel me to pull the trigger and make the trade? I really didn't *need* another fountain pen.

There is something seductive about a fountain pen: the feel of the nib as it glides across paper, the balance of the pen, and the flow of ink. Men like Alexandre Dumas, preferred this tactile experience, as with quills, as he penned in whole or part 250 novels, including *The Count of Monte Cristo,* and *The Three Musketeers.* One can imagine Twain, with his Conklin fountain pen, presenting life on the Mississippi and creating Huckleberry Finn and Tom Sawyer. Or, perhaps, imagine F. Scott Fitzgerald, as he paints the great American novel, *The Great Gatsby,* with fountain pen upon a paper canvas.

CONTENT **OR COVETOUS**

What it boils down to, when it's distilled to its essence, essentially has nothing to do with fountain pens, per se, but the conflict between being content and being covetous.

My wife is almost always content, perhaps as much as any mere mortal could be. I once gave her diamond earrings. It was our first anniversary (the same year I got myself/she got me the Waterman). She prefers bean burritos to diamonds, for real, simple bean burritos with green sauce, sour cream, and onions. She never wears the earrings, perhaps she traded them for hundreds of specialty burritos, but she would never do that. She did accept a nice pen once, a roller ball pen that matched my Coliseum fountain pen. She likes the pen, because she appreciates the artistry, but she never *needed* the pen. We haven't seen that pen for awhile, and she fears she lost it. I doubt she's trying to cover-up a scheme where she traded for more burritos. Content people are free from those terrors.

I was in Nairobi, Kenya, once. There is tremendous poverty in Africa, and in Nairobi it is on full display. Many live in simple shacks with tin roofs: a tin roof and small wood/coal burning stove for cooking and heating. Improper ventilation covers the 150-square-foot room with soot. The soot is noticeable everywhere, seemingly noticeable on the dirt floor. This is in essence a typical home. Yet, there is the pervasive spirit of hospitality. Kenyans inform you that you must visit, and so you do. Perhaps, arriving at 10:00 a.m. (time is almost irrelevant) you are served chai (really just black tea with abundant quantities of sugar and evaporated milk]) and you sit and talk. My "western-mind" and personality compel me to occasionally look at my watch. I tell them that I must be going [now the third time I have tried to excuse myself] as it is almost noon. I'm advised that I *must* stay, because my hosts have prepared lunch. I agree/relent and accept the gracious invite. Lunch is served: the chai is refilled, and there is toast with butter and honey. Tears well-up in my eyes and I fight them back, afraid to embarrass myself or dishonor my hosts. They have presented *all* the food in the house. There was no holding back, no pretense, only love, smiles, and contentment that radiated like diamonds on black velvet.

I want contentment, I want to be generous. I have a friend who is a wonderful, godly woman. She and her husband have three daughters. They needed a car, and at the time could not afford one. I told her she could use mine. She asked, "What will you drive?" I told her we have an extra car, and insisted she use the car. She tells me it's a blessing, and considers my gesture noble. Perhaps it is, but it would have been truly noble if I didn't have a spare, if I truly sacrificed. Could I be content enough to give 'til it hurt? Yet, if I was truly content it would not hurt, only satisfy.

WHERE **TO FIND CONTENTMENT**

You can't "legislate" contentment. That should seem obvious, but consider with me the following: It is said that there are 613 commandments in the Mosaic Law. Only 10 were written with the "finger of God." Presumably, they are extremely important to govern God's people. Now imagine that you have the task to write the municipal code for a new city, and you only get 10 laws to regulate the city. What rules would you choose? Perhaps stealing, murder, and paying taxes come to mind. It is difficult to imagine regulating people with only 10 rules. I have heard it said that there are more words used by the Federal Government to regulate the sale of cauliflower, than were used in the entire Declaration of Independence (I haven't counted to verify this report).

If you only had 10 rules, chances are you wouldn't include coveting. Yet, God does, because He understands how dangerous this insidious condition can be. The god of materialism has been enthroned in our culture. We build shrines to materialism, dubbing them malls. In my city, we have Premium Outlet Malls. People flock there on weekends, even busloads of tourist shoppers. It is an amazing spectacle, to see people file out of a bus and begin to take pictures of family members standing in front of the stores. I imagine them showing their friends and neighbors pictures from the family vacation, "Here's the ocean, and oh, here we are at Timberland, and look there's Sid in front of Calvin Klein."

C. H. Spurgeon, an influential and oft-quoted pastor of another century, once remarked, "If you're not content with what you have, you won't be with twice as much." Money is not the root of all evil, but *the love of money* is. Why? Perhaps countless reasons, but in particular, Jesus said, "You cannot serve God and money," it's impossible. Jesus did not mandate that we give all our earthly possessions away and live in a cave as a means to contentment. Nevertheless, materialism is a dangerous master.

Jesus is the most content person I can imagine. He had no home, one change of clothes, and said we'd be happier giving than receiving (and He meant it, He wasn't being cliché). My friend Jay recently told me that he met Mother Teresa, face to face, one on one. It was 20 years ago when he inadvertently bumped into her in an orphanage in Tijuana, Mexico. Mother Teresa grasped the contentment that Jesus spoke of. When Jay told me about meeting her, the hairs on his arm stood up, seemingly a standing ovation in honor of an inspiring person who got it. She appropriated the truth that things will never bring contentment.

I've been around long enough to discover that you can't truly buy happiness, but I've also tried to rent it for awhile. It never really works. Ironically, the new fountain pen is engraved with a signature, *F. Scott Fitzgerald,* the author of *The Great Gatsby*. In his story, Nick Carraway narrates his experience with a host of characters, including Jay Gatsby. Nick concludes in lament of the emptiness and moral decay. The American dream has become corrupted and reduced to the mere pursuit of wealth. Though Gatsby's ability to transform his dreams to reality is what makes him "great," Nick realizes that the era of dreams, both Gatsby's and the American Dream, is over. Wealth, things, and people can never satisfy.

Well, it seems that it's time to put the cap back on this fountain pen, but before I do, one last reflection on contentment. David penned the 23rd Psalm, perhaps with a primitive fountain pen, but that doesn't really matter. He was at the end of his life, a full life rich with experience. As he reflected, he began, "The Lord is my shepherd; I shall not want." I have discovered this simple truth: when I allow the Lord to be my shepherd, I am content, satisfied, and I do not want.

CHAPTER EIGHT

GENNEX

[HOPE AND THE NEXT GENERATION]

COMING **OF AGE**

Ever wonder what the world will be like for the next generation? Sometimes, I wonder how they will change the world, and whether it will be for better or for worse. I marvel at the experience of being a parent. Karen and I have been blessed with two boys, and as they are now 13 and 10, I guess it's appropriate to say two sons. The transition toward adulthood makes me wonder. I wonder about what they will become and who they will be. What will their challenges be? What will their trials and triumphs look like? How will their dreams change? How will their dreams be fulfilled, and which ones will be crushed? Dreams and fairytales are often easily destroyed by life. Life can be a force like a tsunami that destroys things in its path. I don't only think about what *they* will be like, but I'm curious about what their *world* will look like.

I doubt it's any easier with girls. I wouldn't trade my boys for anything or anyone, but I really do think little girls are special. If I had a little girl, she would probably have me wrapped around her finger, just like her mama, my lovely Karen, does. Little girls are so cute. Their clothes are cute, the way they decorate their rooms is cute, and the way they talk is cute. I love little girl diaries, although I concede that I've never been invited to read one and I've never presumed the liberty of intruding.

I've seen the adorable pink diaries with the tab lock and the little key with a heart-shaped pattern. I imagine the developmental stages: from Disney princess; to "boys are stupid"; to "I'm crushing on this boy, and I think he likes me"; to ... Then diaries stop. Young girls morph and diaries become journals. Older, teen girls and their more mature female counterparts pen journals. Journals reflect the transition from girl to young woman, superficial to deep, and from self-conscious to social conscience. Shallow, selfish little girls in big-girl bodies don't pour their souls into journals. They may write selfish, shallow little thoughts in a journal simply because at 17 it may be awkward to buy a pink Cinderella diary at Borders.

However, for all intents and purposes, they may have just as well written in a pink plastic diary with a crayon, there is nothing for me to connect with emotionally.

On the other hand, a young woman of substance could write in a pink plastic diary with a crayon, fountain pen, or ballpoint and I'd be compelled to connect. To see a young person wrestle with the meaning of social issues, deep philosophical issues, and the meaning of life is bittersweet. They have discovered that the world is a place where fairytales don't always come true. It seems that soon after they have graduated to journals, young women are walked down the aisle by their father as he tries to hold back a flood of tears, afraid to lose his composure, afraid to lose her. He not only fears losing her to the groom who anxiously awaits her hand, but fears losing "his little girl" to a world that can be cold and cruel.

One wonders not only what the world will look like in the sense of how things will be different, but how will the next generation shape and change the world. What will their influence be? What does the future hold for "Generation Next" the generation that holds the future?

Who is the next generation? "Generation X" is a term generally used to describe the post-Baby Boomer generation in the United States. "Generation Y" is a term generally used to describe the group born after "Gen X" and are typically defined as being born about 1980 or later. "Gen Ys" are also described as Echo Boomers, Millennials, and the Internet Generation. The MTV generation may be used to describe a cusp group born between the two [i.e., 1975-1985]. "Generation Z" as you may surmise, are the kids following the "Ys." The demographers' labels: Echo Boomers, Millennials, Internet Generation, MTV Generation, and Generation Z, may or may not be embraced by those being described. Therefore, with all respect, and in sincere hope that I do not offend, I have generically referred to them as "GenNex."

A significant demographic shift is likely to occur in 2011 when the oldest Boomers hit retirement age [65+]. As Boomers shift positions in the workforce, more Gen X members will assume roles in middle and upper management. In addition, Gen Y members will assume the majority of positions in the lower half of the workforce. These shifts are already in process. This trend has some social commentators concerned because of perceived traits regarding GenNex.

One of the primary concerns appears to be a perception of being rebellious or rude. Really, GenNex members are often perceived as not recognizing authority in the same way as prior generations. There is perhaps concern that GenNex will destroy the status quo and wreck the whole system. I, for one, because of my anti-institutional leanings, am not opposed to the status quo being shaken up, but that's another story.

Let me share some observed trends that raise concern and paint a bleak picture. Underage drinking and illegal drug use is prevalent among high school and college age members of GenNex. Second, this generation is facing higher costs for education. Third, a recent survey in Australia showed that business owners perceive them as, "demanding, impatient, and bad at communicating." Finally, although they believe in God and speak to Him, many have no idea who He really is.

REASONS **FOR HOPE**

Let me offer some insights regarding some GenNexers I know that may brighten the picture, and may reflect hope for their generation.

First there is Mari, the oldest of the young people I'd like to tell you about. I got to know her as she and her fiancé Jason were preparing to get married. Mari was working at a high-end jeweler, the kind of place where people drop plastic for a birthday present that would take a working bloke a half a year to earn. Yet, she has a degree in children's education.

Mari is warm, hospitable, and essentially adorable: she's cute, with a dynamite smile, and every time I see her she's got a new hair style, always making a fashion statement. If I had a little girl, I'd get her a "Mari doll" and my little girl would dress her up, do her hair and perfect makeup, and be creative with her, just like the real Mari. I bet my little girl would have the Mari doll make a difference in the world. She'd pretend that the Mari doll would quit working at the jewelry store (after the Christmas season, and after plenty of responsible notice). Then the Mari doll would start working with children and would help train other teachers to show them how to love and help the kids too. My little girl would have her Mari doll be so virtuous, that when friends were "losing it" Mari would come to their house, along with Jason, who would have to tag along like Ken in Barbie's world, and Mari would just be there to comfort them.

Little girls can be so idealistic in their fairytale little worlds. Yet, dreams do come true; Mari did, and continues to do, all of the above. Mari is hard-working, kind, and compassionate. If only we could clone her or manufacture the Mari doll.

Then there's Zach [aka Zach Mc, Z-Mac, Z, and Mac]. With all those nicknames, the mind tends to default toward gangsta-rap icons, but erase all the images, and replace them with their opposite [more like Clark Kent]. Zach is one of my favorite young people, because of his depth of soul and his ability to reflect and ponder meaningful issues. His friend Lauren is a young lady that I've known since she was a little girl playing on my kitchen floor with pots on her head. Lauren is a gifted singer, and could likely play the lead in a Disney movie about young people in a musical. Yet, as much as she might like the role in some sense, she would want to turn it down as being too superficial; I love that conflict. Lauren can talk like a babbling brook, and that's a good thing, especially since

Zach can seem to be a dry well.

Zach has plenty going on his head, but generally spends more time listening and observing. I've been to three working factories in my life, and each time was impressed by the activity going on inside the veiled exterior of the building. I imagine that if I could crawl inside of Zach's ear, that is what I'd see going on inside his head - impressive activity. Zach was a journalist, and planned to be a sports writer (he's a gifted athlete too). He's a college student that spends a great deal of his waking hours trying to provoke his peers to consider some of the weightier issues of life, and he's been successful in his efforts.

One of my favorite days was going to an afternoon baseball game with Zach. We both love the game and our beloved Dodgers. One of the beauties of the game of baseball is its pace. Some might accuse the game of being boring, but I praise the game for the perfection of its pace, for its tempo allows for conversation. On many an occasion, the conversation can be benign inquiries about the game at hand. For example, "Do you think he's gonna steal second?" But, on this occasion, I got to hear the mind, heart, and soul of Zach. Baseball tickets can be expensive, but this day was priceless. Zach provides an abundance of reasons to have hope in GenNex.

Justin D. is another character who is a delight to me simply because he is not "a character." Justin [JD] is a college student, and one of the traits I enjoy so much about him is his humility. Justin is a bass player, he's really cute, has excellent manners, and he is so selfless. He's a great listener. I once asked him, "Justin how do you want to influence your world?" Most young people tell me about some ambitious plan to cure cancer or the like. I'm sure it's noble and well intentioned, but I was really moved by Justin's answer, "I just want to love people." Such a simple answer, but so profound and inspiring! Justin never seems to promote himself, but he's sincere, and seems to just want to care for others. If a primary allegation is that GenNex is rude, rebellious, and selfish then Justin is a poster child for hope.

Trevor is another young person who fans the flames of optimism in GenNex. Trevor was quarterback on the high school football team, and by many accounts a rather good one. The QB is effectively a field general, he receives commands from headquarters, but on the battlefield of the gridiron he directs the offensive assault. When he graduated from high school he had the option to play football in college, albeit in a less than prestigious school where he would not likely be seen on national TV. He declined, and chose instead to pursue more altruistic endeavors.

I watch the wrestling match going on inside of Trev. He's an aggressive QB who wants to march the ball down the field and score on the opening possession. An impatient QB is likely to throw interceptions if he tries to force something to happen when there isn't really an opening. The great ones learn to bridle the impulse, be patient, and to wait for the game of life to unfold in its natural order, and for openings to arise. Trevor is really trying to help others, and do the right thing in life, and that's commendable. He wants to make a difference and make things happen now, but he is also learning to be patient.

Then there is one young lady who is extremely special to me ...

FUTURE **TENSE**

Her name is Julianne, a melodic name that flows like a one-word song. If I have ever a daughter, I want her to be (like) Julianne, an affirmation I have declared to her on countless occasions. For as each of these young people (and I assure you there are more) have given me hope in the next generation, perhaps no one else can compare to Julie. It is not that she is greater or more esteemed than the others I have told you about, because each of them has a special room in my heart. But Julianne has a whole estate reserved in my heart. For when she was just a little toe-head girl, she came into my life. Since then, she has just been adding rooms, year by year, so that now she occupies an estate.

At this point, you might wonder what makes her so special that she has been given the privilege of setting up such a large residence in my heart. It would seem almost cruel and twisted to refuse to tell you, so I will. The earliest images of her are preserved in a framed collage, along with pictures of my sons as young boys. Julie is about ten, and she is holding our youngest when he was about two. Johnny has blond hair and green Osh Kosh overalls that bring out the green in Julianne's eyes. Her blond hair makes her look like an older sister, and she is holding "her little brother." She has a huge smile, like someone who went sleepwalking through a closet and swallowed a hanger. In a few years, she would be my boys' favorite babysitter.

A few more years would pass, and Julianne was in high school. She played on the girl's basketball team, learned to play guitar, and was overflowing with compassion. That year, we were on a mission trip to Mexico with a group from our church. She showered mercy and love upon all the kids we encountered. The little girl had grown up to be a beautiful young lady, and I knew that she was going to break hearts.

A couple of more years passed and she was leading worship for the high school group at church. Her Mom, Christine, is a worship leader, and the apple doesn't fall far from the tree. Julie was shy and reserved, and had not yet grown into the gifts that God had given her, like a child when they first ride a bike without training wheels. But, soon she would stand on the platform "in the big church" before many adults, and close her eyes and strike her first guitar chord, and sing to God. As she sang praise to Him, there was a sense that she had entered the very presence of God, and we wanted to follow her there. Her voice was strong, like a clarion call harkening us to prepare our hearts, because God was here. There was authority, and there was depth. Our little girl had become a young woman.

THE MYSTERY OF INVESTING

Julie allowed me a peek into her journal to read a story she wrote that reflects who she is, what she thinks, and depth beyond her years. I think it's encouraging to consider as we contemplate GenNex. She graciously allowed me to share it with you. She calls it, *The Mystery of Investing*:

There are quite a few things that I do not understand, like the mystery of investing. Recently, I opened a credit card account at the bank. Since then, my account has gotten smaller. The reason is obvious: I now have an all-access pass to the money in my account and can charge my card whenever I want. In the same way, I can invest whenever I want, but I don't. If I simply invested more than I withdrew, my life would be richer.

What happens when a person goes to withdraw money from the bank and their account is empty? The person is left empty handed. What happens if a person charges their credit card and is unable to pay the bank because they have no money left in their account? The person gets hit with fines! She may not even have known her account was empty until she is hit with reality when the bill comes.

Over the past few weeks, I discovered my spiritual bank account was empty. I did not get hit with fines and have to repay it all; however, in time of need or desire when I wanted to use my spiritual credit card and call on God, I was unable to withdraw. But isn't God ALWAYS there for us? Isn't God the one who is ALWAYS faithful? Yes, God was faithfully there for me. However, my encounter with Him during those times was shallow. It is true that when I faced a trial and turned to God that He was there. Yet, I could only go so far. Why? Because my account had run dry. I had told God I no longer needed Him when I refused to invest. God wanted to be there for me, but I couldn't receive the love from Him that I had discovered while investing in Him. Despite the all access pass to all that I invested in God, I had withdrawn my investment and failed to replace it.

During times when I had invested in the Lord, I could easily see my need for Him. I could see how He was the one who was filling my account. Yet, over time, that need slowly slipped to the back of my mind. It got to the point that I no longer saw my need to invest in the Lord. For some time, I had been withdrawing from my spiritual bank account. I would use the credit card when I needed it, but I failed when it came to actually investing. God was what I needed in the hard times. When I messed up and needed mercy, I withdrew. When I was in a situation where a servant was needed, I withdrew. When I was angry at someone and needed love, I withdrew. These are all good things to withdraw. The problem is, the more I withdrew, the less I invested. The time I actually spent with God to get to know Him and the time I spent praising Him was minimal in comparison to the time I took out of His riches. How could I have been so naïve to think that I could invest nothing but keep withdrawing?

Investing is hard. Like putting money in the bank instead of spending right away, it requires sacrifice. There are also benefits to a credit card. Money keeps us alive by providing food and shelter and many other things. If a person only invested but NEVER withdrew, they would have no way to make it through life. In the same way, God WANTS us to withdraw from Him. If all we did in our walk with God was invest but never take out of Him, our lives would be dry because we would be depending on ourselves. God loves to shower us with His blessings of love, kindness and mercy *because we discover all those things about God while investing.*

I came to a conclusion. I decided that instead of spending my time investing in other things and withdrawing from God, I would invest in God and withdraw from God. This didn't mean that I had to stop investing in other things; it meant that while I could still invest in other people, ultimately, I had to invest in God above all of these things. My time should be prioritized with God always first.

How do we get back to this first love? Well, we lose our first love when we forget our need for Him. True love is unconditional: love that expects nothing in return. This is how God loves us. I had to do the same. This meant I needed to invest, but not for the sole sake of being able to withdraw. God wanted me to invest because through investing, we know God and see His love for us and our need for Him. I longed for that simple faith of just loving God to know Him, and not to get something from Him. I know full well that God will always come through. I have never doubted that. Yet, I had become so caught up in withdrawing from God that I failed to invest. I think I've begun to solve the mystery of investing.

Julianne's story inspires me and gives me hope. She and a countless number of her peers, including Mari, Zach, Lauren, JD, and Trev, are wrestling with the deep significant issues of life. GenNexers are often very spiritual and are devoted to such things as a confident belief in God and a commitment to a life of prayer. Many are finding meaning and a life worth living as they come to truly know God and make Him known. I praise GenNexers' energy and charisma, and I'm excited about their opportunity to make the world better.

As I reflect upon *The Mystery of Investing* I consider not only my investments and withdrawals with God, but how am I investing into others. What is my responsibility to the next generation? What is my responsibility to invest my time, my energy, and my heart?

Do I really know people in GenNex and their struggles, concerns, triumphs and tragedies? Have I made the effort to listen to what makes them angry about me and my generation without trying to defend or justify? Have I discovered what they are afraid of? Have I helped them to connect and learn valuable lessons from the generation before them? Have I helped them to meet the real Jesus?

As I contemplate GenNex, I remain optimistic that they will make the world a better place. There are many I know who inspire me and give me hope. Yet, I can't help but wonder what example I am giving. What impressions am I imparting, and what thoughts would they record if they wrote in their journal a paragraph to summarize my influence.

CHAPTER NINE

ARTICHOKES

[CAN WE BE VULNERABLE IN RELATIONSHIPS?]

PROTECTED **HEART**

Why is it so hard to be vulnerable in relationships? Perhaps surprisingly, I've learned much about vulnerability from artichokes. In 1948 Marilyn Monroe, then Norma Jeane Baker, was crowned Castroville's first "Artichoke Queen." Castroville is the artichoke center of the world. For five decades they have hosted the artichoke festival. The vegetable thrives in the cool coastal climate of California's Monterey County. The festival features a carnival atmosphere, competitions for premier artichokes, and agro art (three-dimensional fruit and vegetable artwork, a quirky competition that is intended to foster creativity, imagination, and fun for contestants and viewers alike). The main event is the food, and the star of the show is the artichoke. There are mouthwatering recipes such as: artichoke crab dip, cream of artichoke soup, marinated artichoke hearts, pizza topped with artichoke hearts, and French-fried artichoke. The artichoke surprisingly yields a brilliant purple flower that hints at its royalty, and also unexpected discovery.

The experience of eating artichokes together can be intimate. My wife loves artichokes. She enjoys eating them with melted butter or mayonnaise, and likes to season them (I would reveal the secret seasoning to you, but I may be required to delete at least one of the spices to preserve the secret, and that would likely defeat the purpose of telling you). In late spring artichokes are in season, and they are abundant, and inexpensive. Karen, always the savvy shopper, waits for the price to decline, and then pounces like a cat upon its prey. Soon our home is filled with the aroma of artichokes.

We sit at the table and begin to partake in the artichoke ritual. To enjoy an artichoke one must respect the process. You remove outer leaves that tend to be tougher, and dip in an appropriate sauce, and then enjoy the wonderful taste and texture. Each concentric layer of leaves becomes softer as you journey to the heart. As you are now yearning to partake of this delicacy, I must warn you that there are points at the end of each leaf, and these can prick the skin. I assume that at finer dining establishments they remove the points for you before serving. Although my wife is a wonderful cook, she does not provide this service. Fortunately, the points are not life threatening, but are generally simply annoying and uncomfortable. Nevertheless, the delicate and rich artichoke heart beckons at the center of the artichoke, surrounded by the protective shell of outer pointed leaves.

As Karen and I share an artichoke, we remove the outer leaves, dip and partake, and we talk. Karen, well trained in protocol and etiquette, does not speak with her mouth full, unlike her seemingly boorish husband. All the while we work toward the heart together and prepare to partake of its goodness.

Artichokes, like much of life, are seasonal. Much of the world measures seasons by changes in the weather. Falling snow gives way to melting ice, blades of new green grass and vibrant wildflowers, flowing streams and waterfalls, long days, warm lakes, berries, and then falling leaves – autumn's golden colors. Each year, the cycle unfolds with rhythmic patterns signaling change, growth, and dormancy. On the other hand, in Southern California we measure seasons by the calendar in our ever-sunny world. Alas, as the Arabic proverb foretells: too much sunshine can make a desert. Therefore, in life one must be careful: the pursuit of sunshine and happiness, and the avoidance of rain, can reduce an oasis to a barren wasteland. A heart that is too protected, that only seeks sunshine and happiness, and avoids rain and pain, can become lifeless. Therefore, we must learn to become vulnerable. Seasons of life are sometimes measured by relationship, genuine relationships characterized by vulnerability. People come into your life for seasons and for reasons.

HEART **SURGERY**

My seasons are often signaled by quarterly reminders in my electronic calendar. Recently there was a reminder popping up in my seemingly ever present PDA advising me that a new season had arrived. Another opportunity for change, a new season for growth — four cryptic bullet points:

• Too gracious
• Need to listen better
• Don't work so hard
• Be less attorney-like

What could those words possibly have to do with artichokes? Presumably nothing, but one cannot be too sure. Perhaps we should investigate further.

These bullet points were directed to someone's heart. Over a course of time, relationship had taken place such that the outer protective leaves had been progressively removed. Now these pointed bullets took aim at the heart. Were they simply words, ideas, concerns, or criticism? Would they travel through the last tender leaves, and pierce the heart? Who was the target, and who pulled the trigger, and who took aim with these bullets? Were they truly aimed at the heart or the mere random spray of bullets from some sociopath bent on destruction?

The words had been first shared six months before, or two seasons ago. For the next two seasons, each three months, these bullets would appear at the scene. Perhaps they would kill something that needed to die, but could they possibly give life at the same time? These bullet points represent an opportunity: a chance to consider, grow, ponder, reflect, and to change. Seasons of life should bring change.

The insights had been provided to me by my dear friend Roger

– Lynn's husband. She is a moral compass, but that's another story. Roger is one of the people who gives hope for mankind. He is one of the few that I've never heard anyone say anything negative about. Roger is loyal, faithful, caring and fun. He's like one of those golden retrievers that want to play and catch Frisbees. One of those cool dogs that never have to be put on a leash because they don't run after cats, bite people, or do other things they're not supposed to do. He'd be like that golden retriever that hangs out, patiently waiting outside a coffee house, wearing his bandana, and never having to be on a leash. The kind of dog that everyone approaches to pet, because they're not afraid of him; and they know that they'll be comforted by simply coming in contact with him.

Roger is a great friend, the kind of person you'd call at midnight when you're having a car emergency. He's also fun to hang with. He's a surfer and a "baller." Most guys who surf or skateboard aren't guys who necessarily like ball sports like football, baseball, or basketball, but Roger's down with it all. He's one of those handy guys who can do all sorts of construction projects, and still has all ten fingers. He's also one of those "relationship" people that like to go out for a meal, and sit and talk. His favorite kind of food is whatever someone else is buying; but no one ever minds taking him out for lunch, because he is so genuinely interested in other people. He is one of the only people I've ever met that I thought could be the director of a kid's camp and a counselor for adults.

Roger is gentle, but firm. He would never want to hurt anyone, but he is also loving enough to be sincere and to tell the truth, even when it's something that someone doesn't necessarily want to hear. He is extremely wise. One day, I remember Roger talking to a friend of ours. Roger had tried to help him see that he had a character issue that had to be dealt with. Our friend said, "I've been praying about what you said, but God hasn't spoken to me about that." Roger gently responded, "What if God is speaking to you right now through me."

VULNERABLE HEART

It was shortly after that incident, that I asked Roger, "Where do I need to grow?" Roger is many wonderful things, but to me, he is my friend and "accountability partner." I'm not really sure what the term accountability partner implies, but it seems descriptive of this aspect of our relationship. As I reflect back, it wasn't something that I really planned, considered, or thought through. I simply desired to grow personally and spiritually, and wanted to discover areas where I needed to consider change. So, I asked my friend the simple, but poignant question, "Where do I need to grow?"

It seems that God designed us with a desire to be open and honest with others. This appears to be God's ideal for relationships. In the very beginning of God's story, there is vulnerability and no sin. Adam and Eve are in the Garden of Eden, they are naked, and unashamed. When I first read that story, I figured they weren't ashamed because they probably had awesome bodies. Eve probably looked like the sculpture of Venus, only with arms, and Adam probably looked like he did about 1,000 push-ups and sit-ups a day. Later, I realized that when God made trees, they already had fruit on them. In other words, they had the appearance of age from their very first day. I began to think that maybe Adam and Eve didn't have super bodies. Maybe they had the appearance of age. Maybe Adam was losing his hair, and combing it over like some congressman on C-SPAN, and perhaps Eve had a little cellulite on her thighs.

I began to consider that they weren't ashamed because of how they looked; rather they weren't ashamed because sin had not yet entered the world. They were completely vulnerable, and comfortable with each other. I imagine a conversation in the Garden at that time. Eve asks Adam, "Honey, where do I need to grow?" Adam replies, "You're perfect honey. You're the only woman for me!" And he means it!

Then, I turn the page to the next chapter in God's story.

Adam and Eve have been tempted, fallen, and sin has entered the Garden. Immediately, there is a sense of shame. Adam and Eve immediately try to cover themselves in fig leaves. They are no longer vulnerable. Adam and Eve have been separated from God because of their rebellion. As a result, they are less vulnerable with each other.

I imagine that their conversations changed. Eve looked at herself in the fig leaves, and somewhat shyly asked Adam, "Does this make me look fat?" Adam coldly replied, "No, you look fat in everything!" Eve was hurt, and thought to herself, "I'll never ask that question again. I'll never let him hurt me like that." She began to build up layers of protection around her tender heart, like an artichoke. She was afraid of being hurt, and of being judged. Adam perceives that Eve seems more distant, less approachable, less intimate, but he doesn't know what to do about it. So he simply and cynically concludes, "I guess this is how it will be from now on." Things looked pretty grim in the Garden.

If God wants us to be vulnerable and intimate with Him as well as with one another, why is it so difficult? I ask friends that question, and I learn some great insights. First, many of us have never really thought about being vulnerable. For most of us the primary obstacles are fear, pride and shame. To become vulnerable means that I can be hurt and that you may judge me. Intimacy is risky business. It is frightening to think that you might rain on my parade, but somehow I also understand that too much sunshine makes a desert.

Yet, there is something very cleansing about rain, and the growth it brings. Personal growth is exciting, but it generally requires vulnerability. What helps us to become vulnerable? People tell me they want trust, respect, and knowing that someone cares. Most of all, they want an example, but where can you find real and healthy vulnerability?

One of the great stories of the Bible is the scene where Jesus gathered with His followers to observe the Passover meal, only hours before He went to the cross [John 13]. In that culture, it was customary for a servant to wash the feet of the master's dinner guests. This was common hospitality, like we would offer a guest something to drink. None of the disciples offered to wash the feet of the other guests. So, Jesus removed His garments and began to wash the disciples' feet. At first, the disciples protested the idea of Jesus washing their feet, but Jesus explained that it was necessary. The lesson was not simply about serving others, but is a wonderful example of being vulnerable.

When Jews, like the disciples, arrived at Jerusalem for the Passover feast, they would participate in ceremonial baths to cleanse themselves. These ritual baths were a symbol of the spiritual cleansing that God wants to do in our hearts. From the ceremonial baths, they would walk the dirt streets, in open sandals, to the place where they would eat the Passover meal. In the process, their feet would become dirty.

Jesus wanted His followers to realize that they had dirt that needed to be cleansed. When anyone asks Jesus into their life, and chooses to follow Him, God will forgive them, and they are clean before Him. Yet, as we walk through life, there is still dirt to deal with. Sometimes we are reluctant to discover that we are dirty, and to try to clean-up. The disciples didn't need a bath, they needed spot-cleansing. As Jesus washed their feet He was in contact with them, and, presumably, He applied just the right pressure. I imagine that He did not rub so hard that He removed their skin, and I'm sure that He didn't leave the dirt on them. Similarly, I assume the water temperature was just right, not ice cold, nor boiling hot. Jesus made them as comfortable as possible. He was vulnerable and so were they. And the result was that He made them completely clean.

Spiritual growth is like removing dirt. There are issues in our lives that need to be removed, but it requires vulnerability. Foot washing can be an awkward experience. Feet can be unpleasant for a number of reasons. It is often very embarrassing to be vulnerable and expose your feet to someone else. Yet, if we are willing, others can help us clean-up and grow-up. How can we be vulnerable so that we can grow?

GETTING TO THE HEART

Vulnerability is like eating artichokes: it is a process. Relationships and friendships are the way to remove tough outer leaves. For me, it began by realizing my friend cared about me, we respected each other, that he would try not to hurt me, and that he could help me grow. Then, the simple question, "Where do I need to grow?" Instantly, more outer leaves were removed, and my heart was exposed. Remember, artichokes have sharp points that can annoy, and even draw a little blood, but they are seldom or ever lethal. When you ask someone where you need to grow, sometimes the reply can irritate. I needed to listen, not "point back," and let the words reach my heart.

Roger was honest and loving and shared his heart with me:

- Too gracious
- Need to listen better
- Don't work so hard
- Less attorney-like

Those bullet points represent issues in my life that I need to consider in order to change and grow. Every three months, I review the list with Roger, and I ask my friend, "How am I doing?" We talk about each item and whether I'm growing, getting worse, or staying the same. Then I ask if there are any new items that we need to add to the list. Occasionally, we agree that it's time to take an item off the list.

As much as Roger and my other friends help me grow, I realize that only Jesus can really clean me. My job is to be vulnerable. I'm to create relationships where my friends can point out that I'm dirty; and I'm to be willing to allow Jesus to transform me and make me clean. Similarly, I'm to learn to help my friends see where they are dirty, and help them discover the cleansing that is available. That whole dynamic can sometimes feel like eating artichokes.

Artichokes have a limited season, and then the opportunity to partake is gone. The Greeks use two different words to describe time. *Kronos* describes measurable intervals of time such as minutes and hours. *Kairos* measures opportunities or seasons. Kairos was depicted as a winged "cherub" with a predominantly bald head with the exception of a long ponytail. As Kairos passed by, one had to grab the ponytail or it was gone. Seasons and opportunities tend to pass. Some of us wisely reach out and receive, but others miss out on the opportunities. While you have the opportunity, look to develop relationships where you can be vulnerable, relationships like artichokes. Bon Appetit!

CHAPTER TEN

DIVINE
APPOINTMENTS

[KEEPING THE MOST IMPORTANT MEETINGS]

SYNCHRONIZED **CALENDARS**

Do you really know what your most important appointments are? I hate to miss appointments. I always have my PDA (personal digital assistant) nearby. I almost treat it like an umbilical cord. If I don't have my calendar and contacts nearby during all my waking hours I might die. To insure my viability, all my appointments are synchronized in the computer as a backup to the handheld PDA. One can't be too careful you know.

There have been some appointments that fell through the cracks, maybe more than I realize. On the other hand, there have been some appointments that I've kept that I never even scheduled and didn't even know I had. These may have been the best appointments of all.

A couple of years ago, I got a call from a man early Monday morning. I didn't know the man, but we go to the same church. He asked if he could come by to talk to me. Generally, my schedule is so full, that appointments are backed up for several weeks. However, this Monday I had two hours free. So I told him, "If you can get here right now, I'm available." He said, "I'll see you in 10 minutes." Ten minutes later, he came rolling into my office ... I don't mean metaphorically, but literally. He introduced himself as David and he was in a wheelchair. So far, that's all I knew.

I asked, "How can I help you?" It was a generic question, but I hoped that it didn't sound patronizing to a man in a wheelchair. He responded, "I'm not exactly sure." So I asked, "Why are you here?" David began to explain that while he was at church on Sunday, the day before, he had a sense that God was telling Him, "Go and speak with this guy" [i.e. me]. Then, about five minutes later, his wife leaned over, and whispered to him, "I think God wants you to go talk with that guy." Therefore, he simply decided to be obedient and came to meet with me, but he had no idea why.

I asked him to tell me what was going on, and he simply began to share with me about his journey. David had been injured in an accident about two years before. As a result, he was paralyzed from the waist down. It was two long years of adjusting physically, emotionally, and spiritually. David had wrestled and played football before his injury, and he looks like Mr. Incredible. However, being paralyzed can presumably mess with your mind and soul, as well as your body.

David was preparing to return to the workforce, but he would not be returning to his former employer. He figured maybe that's why God brought him to talk to me to figure out what God was doing regarding those issues. So I asked David, "What do you want to do? What have you done?" David has been a finance guy, "CPA, MBA, and CFO – type." He began to tell me about his background and experience, and I began to realize that this was going to be a very special, albeit unscheduled, appointment.

The preceding Friday, the church pastors had met with the church business administrator. He was going to be leaving his administrator position to pastor a brand-new church. We talked about a transition plan, and agreed that we would talk more in a week. Meanwhile, only the pastors and the business administrator knew that a position would be available. David had no idea.

The church needed a finance guy, and David was looking to re-enter the workforce. I'm not the sharpest tool in the shed, but even I could see God's fingerprints all over this appointment. The more we talked, the more we realized that our meeting was a divine appointment. God was working in our hearts to bring us together, before we had a clue as to why. Soon thereafter, David was working at the church as the business administrator.

It was obvious that God had brought us together that day, but I also realized there were probably many times that God was working behind the scenes in my life, and I was too busy with my agenda to see.

UNSCHEDULED **APPOINTMENTS**

About a year passed from the day I met David, and I was at the church early one morning when I had another unscheduled appointment. It was Saturday when my friend John came walking by. John and I never see each other on Saturdays at church, and although we both affirm that we're there all the time, we just don't meet. John is an elder at the church and an awesome human being. He works with an international organization that provides wheelchairs to disabled people all over the world. He had been to Africa 10 to 12 times, and I told him that I was going to be going to Kenya soon. At that moment, I sensed that I was supposed to ask John to go with me. As John thought about it, we both knew that it was a "God thing." John and I talked about the plan to help start a Bible teaching church in Nairobi, Kenya, and some of the challenges the trip would likely present.

We both came back to the church that night for a concert and bumped into each other in the parking lot. John told me that he had spoken with his wife, and both of them sensed that he was supposed to go with me to Africa. Then John said, "What do you think about asking David to go with us?" I began to think about it for a moment, and some of the peculiar challenges David would encounter. Africa is not as user friendly for a handicapped person as Southern California. Nevertheless, I sensed that God wanted David to be there. Moments later, David arrived and John and I asked him if he wanted to come with us. At first, David looked surprised, then curious, and then excited. After a few days, David was confirmed, along with John and our friend Tom. Our team was set.

The slums of Nairobi are not an ideal place for a person with a disability. They are densely populated. Mud streets and rain make a bad recipe for a man in a wheelchair and, in this case, a big man. We found ourselves laying boards along the way, and David would roll across, then we would reposition the boards, and continue. One afternoon we were hosting a group of about 100 pastors, and David came forward to speak about ministering to the disabled community.

In much of Africa disabled persons are generally not seen in public. The disabled are perceived as cursed by some deity (e.g. their disability is a result of judgment for some heinous wrong). As a result of this perception, family members hide their disabled relatives. If you were to visit a home where a child had a disability such as Down's syndrome or polio, you would never see the child. They generally would be locked in a room and not allowed out until the visitors left.

Also, Kenyans and most Africans generally require someone to establish their credentials before they will accept what someone claiming some authority has to say. In other words, it would have been typical for David to have been introduced as a speaker with a description of his credentials as a business administrator of a fairly large church, a description of his numerous academic degrees, and a detail of his vocational pedigree. David forsook this introduction. He simply began his address by telling them about playing football, wrestling, weightlifting, and his love for God. He then explained that he had not been cursed, but had simply had an accident. Then he said the clincher, "The only thing that separates me and you, and keeps you from being in a wheelchair, is one accident ..." At that point, every pastor leaned forward to hear every word that David had to say about disabilities ministry.

He asked them, "How many of you still have some empty seats in your sanctuary on Sunday mornings?" Every hand was raised. He then asked, "How many of you would like to fill them?" Every hand was raised. Then he inquired, "How many of you have ever thought of reaching out to the disabled community?" Not a single hand was raised. David then began to explain how people with disabilities actually serve and bless a church. At our church, there are children's ministry workers in wheelchairs. There is a blind man who serves in the children's ministry. We are blessed by greeters in wheelchairs, and a blind man who is a handyman and carpenter. The Kenyan pastors were amazed, impressed, and to say the least interested. Their whole understanding of disabilities had been radically changed.

We realized that not only David, but all the Kenyan pastors who were there that day had a divine appointment. The influence of that meeting has continued and there has actually been a noticeable shift in the community regarding disabled persons. I reflected back to "coincidentally" running into John at the church and sensing that I was supposed to ask him to come to Africa, and how John then sensed that we were supposed to ask David to come. The results of those meetings were profound. I've heard it said that there are no coincidences only "small miracles" where God chose to remain anonymous.

DIVINE APPOINTMENTS

I love divine appointments. They are often unscheduled by us, in whole or in part, but I wouldn't want to miss a single one. One day, several years ago when I was a pre-believer I was looking to move from San Diego to Orange County, California. I was looking at homes in the City of Orange, an area with many older homes full of character and charm. I saw this old brick house built in the 1920s with three arches. A very cool looking house, and very unusual for Southern California (bricks and earthquakes don't mix well). I called the real estate office and an agent named Nick answered and came to show me the house.

Nick is tall and thin (a bike racer), and he is a brilliant thinker with a great sense of humor and a kind heart. He is also a good listener. Nick showed me the house in Orange, and we both concluded that the house wouldn't work for me. So I asked Nick if he could show me some other homes in the area. He readily agreed.

As we drove around, we kept passing a house where the owners had painted "Praise the Lord" in red script letters across the garage. Each time I would make a flippant, sarcastic comment, but Nick wasn't laughing. One time, I made a comment, and Nick looked at me with a hurt look on his face. He explained to me that Jesus was somebody real and important to him. I felt bad, not only that I had offended Nick, but that it must have been gnawing at him for some time. It probably got to the point that he didn't care about possibly losing the likely commission.

Nick was the first person who explained "the gospel" to me. He explained that God loved me and that God was perfect and no one else is. Jesus came to stand in the gap between imperfect man and perfect God. Jesus paid the price for my sin at the cross, proved it by the resurrection, and that I could have a relationship with God. I simply needed to invite Jesus into my life and choose to follow Him.

It seemed reasonable, but too simple, too good to be true. I could accept that I wasn't perfect, a sinner or whatever, and I liked to think that God loved me, but I had other doubts. Not only did I wonder if I wanted to give up certain elements of my life that God probably didn't approve of, but was Jesus really Messiah?

I was born and raised a Jew, and all my life I had heard that Jesus was a good man, a wise rabbi, a learned sage, or a philosopher, but not the Savior of the world. Nick offered me a Bible to read, and invited me to church. It seemed that a decision about Jesus was more significant than changing to a new brand of toothpaste. Not the type of decision to make impulsively, but not the kind of opportunity that I'd want to miss either.

Next Sunday, there I was at church, and it was definitely not like synagogue. First, at synagogue, the men and women were separated by a partition (presumably there would be less distraction at the synagogue). Second, at the synagogue, the cantor would lead the congregation in *a cappella* singing (with many of the songs in Hebrew, which I didn't understand). At the church, the music was also pretty simple just a guy with a guitar and a female vocalist. What was different was how people were responding. At the synagogue, people passively listened. At the church, people were standing up, raising their hands, closing their eyes, and singing to God. They were really seeking to worship God. At first, I just wanted to leave. I'd never experienced that before and I felt like a fish out of water. The immediate problem seemed to be that I was in this very long pew, and I was stuck in the middle! All the "Jesus Freaks" were standing up with their eyes closed on both sides of me. I couldn't escape. There was no way out.

Yet, the more I watched, the more jealous I became. I grew up in the synagogue; I was a Hebrew and these *meshugena* Gentiles loved God more than I did. They really had a relationship with God, while I merely had religion. When the pastor was talking, I must confess I don't remember a lot of what he said. I was looking at my borrowed Bible. I simply opened the book and read; "In the beginning, God created the heavens and the earth ..." I stopped to think about it. If God didn't exist, I didn't need to read the rest of the book, and if He did, I might as well. So I started to check it out. I probably thought I was being gracious by giving God the benefit of the doubt. Like when parents promise something good to their kids and ask, "Do you trust me?" Children generally have some doubts, but are willing to explore an expected good thing.

Interestingly, there was an index in that Bible that had prophecies regarding Messiah from the Old Testament and where the prophecies were fulfilled in the New Testament. There I was sitting in the pew with one finger in the index, one finger in the Old Testament, and one finger in the New Testament. The more I looked, the more I was convinced, that Jesus really was the Messiah. I'd been a trial attorney for years, and had experience in the District Attorney's office. I knew evidence beyond a reasonable doubt, and the case for Christ was becoming increasingly sure.

Nevertheless, I wasn't ready to invite Jesus into my life. But perhaps my meeting with Nick was yet another divine appointment.

MEETING JESUS

The next week, I went to the college and career group at the church. There were a couple of hundred people meeting in a gym. Pastor Bill was about to start a study in the New Testament book of *Hebrews*. As he shared an overview, he explained how the book was written to Jews, who had come to Christ, encouraging them that Jesus was superior to the Mosaic Law because He had fulfilled the Law. As Bill spoke, I realized that this was a divine appointment. It felt like God was tugging on my heart, encouraging me to invite Him in.

Pastor Bill finished the teaching, and asked everyone to close their eyes while he prayed (I have to admit that I peeked). As he prayed he urged, "If anyone would like to invite Jesus into your life tonight raise your hand so that I can pray for you." As I listened to Bill I wanted to raise my hand, but I was afraid. I'd never seen this experience before and I wasn't sure what they would make me do (I assumed religious people could get pretty weird). Some people raised their hands, and the college group leaders distributed cards for people to fill out for later follow-up. As the cards were passed out I again wanted to raise my hand but I didn't.

As I walked to the car I kept thinking that I really wanted to ask Jesus to come into my life and begin a relationship with Him. Once I was in the car I wanted to pray right then and there, but I didn't know the "right words." I assumed that there had to be almost a mystical incantation. Also, I wanted to make sure that it would count without the presence of a bona fide "holy man" such as a priest, rabbi, or pastor. Nevertheless, I was willing to give it a try.

As I think about it today, I have really no idea exactly what I said to God. I probably simply acknowledged that I had come to believe that Jesus really is: the Christ, the Messiah, and the Son of God. And, I knew that my life would be better if I started living it God's way instead of mine. Then, I remember simply asking Jesus to come into my life. I immediately felt an incredible sense of peace. I felt that I had finally discovered what I was searching for all my life, and what could fill the hole inside of me.

Each person has their own journey with God. Therefore, your experience may be different than what I felt that night when I invited Jesus into my heart and began my relationship with God. Nevertheless, I'm confident that you'll agree with me that meeting Jesus is the best appointment ever. Although many years have passed, I've never regretted that divine appointment.

Since then, I've come to appreciate that God moves supernaturally in a seemingly natural way in the circumstances of our lives. I've always tried to be on time, and keep my meetings. But now I try to be more sensitive to God's plans for me. I don't want to be so busy and focused on my agenda that I miss out on what God has planned for me. There are probably countless times that God wanted me to speak to someone, or He sent someone to speak to me and I was too distracted, and I missed a divine appointment. I think we all miss these opportunities more often than we realize. The closer I draw to God, the more I want to be sensitive to His appointments and learn to keep them. They are certainly the most important.

Ironically, I'm currently looking to replace my handheld personal digital assistant and get a new PDA. What I need to remember is to perceive divine appointments ("PDA"). That's a feature I'm not going to find in my highly tech world. I've discovered that when I slow down and spend more time in my relationship with God, I'm more likely to sync my calendar with His and not miss the divine appointments.

CHAPTER ELEVEN

APPLE

[THE MOTIVE ISSUE]

MOTIVE **MATTERS**

I was sitting with my friend Eric at Peet's Coffee, and we were talking about motives for serving God. It is sobering to consider that we can actually be involved in an endeavor like serving others, something potentially pure and noble, and have the wrong heart. Unfortunately when there is heart trouble it takes time for the symptoms to develop and to diagnose the problem. Even then the patient needs to be willing and diligent to receive remedial treatment. If the prescription isn't filled, the patient rarely gets better and often others get infected.

Eric is the tech director at our church. He oversees the sound equipment issues for the worship teams, speakers, and drama presentations. He also supervises video editing and display, projection of song lyrics and speaker's notes, and our sophisticated lighting systems. If that isn't enough he creates most of the graphics that the church uses in a variety of media.

As Eric and I were talking we tried to imagine Jesus' perspective on the multimedia church. Would Jesus be comfortable coming into a multimedia church today? It seems to us, that the most important issue to Jesus would be the heart, or motives, of church leaders. For example, we imagine that Jesus would frown upon performance and production motivated primarily by a leader's desire to attract or entertain people, but He would likely want to communicate with the next generation in their own language. What would Jesus think if He walked into a church with a big dramatic production, light show, (optional fog machine), and well-produced video? It seems so different from Jesus' style of ministry.

I imagine Jesus at the Sea of Galilee speaking to the multitudes the words that we now know as the Sermon on the Mount. It was springtime then. I can picture the green grass, the gentle rolling hills, and the wildflowers in bloom. I assume that Jesus wasn't concerned about distractions caused by fishermen on the lake behind Him, or covering up an unsightly brown patch of grass. He probably wouldn't coordinate a flock of sheep to pass by at a precise time when He planned a dramatic moment in His message, like, "I am the Good Shepherd." He probably wouldn't develop slick flyers with His face posted all over town promoting His "miracle" service. Jesus probably never trained ushers about how to deal with parents and their crying babies, and He probably had never trained professional greeter-types. Those things presumably didn't matter much to Him. Yet, I assume that those things, in and of themselves, are not evil per se. But the issue is motive.

Jesus cares about people. When He looked upon crowds of thousands, He was moved with compassion because He saw them as individuals rather than merely a multitude. He taught them many things about God and, after several hours, He prepared to feed them bread and fish. Obviously, the miracle of feeding more than 5,000 people from only five loaves of bread and two fish is interesting to say the least, but there is another part of that story that also fascinates me. Jesus could have served the food buffet style, but He didn't. Rather, He had the disciples gather the people in groups of about 50 to a 100. Then, Jesus had the disciples feed the people. Why did Jesus have the disciples feed the smaller groups? Perhaps it was to keep order, but I believe there was another reason.

By organizing the people into smaller groups, the disciples would likely appreciate the people as individuals rather than merely a multitude. The disciples would see the individual needs of the people: their poverty, dirty clothes, the effect of the elements and hard labor upon their skin, and the impact of less-than-ideal hygiene conditions. Jesus wants His followers to care about people's needs because that's what He cares about. Jesus is not likely impressed by a show; likewise He isn't trying to impress anyone with a show. Technology is not evil, and can be an extremely effective tool if used with proper motive, but that's the essential issue – motive.

Eric makes a huge impact at our church and has great influence. He is tech-savvy, sharp, incredibly gifted and creative. His graphics are fresh and clean with an edge that attracts youth and others. He is extremely responsible, and diligent. When inspired, he is capable of burning the midnight oil and willing to get up early the next day to finish the job. He does things excellently and works hard at whatever he puts his hand to.

Eric is just finishing college. He's an English major who reads the classics and also loves to read contemporary works, especially books about growing in relationship with God. He has a voracious appetite to learn. His family loves God, and he and his four brothers are all extremely talented and have outstanding character. Eric is fun to be with and is a young man of integrity. He has a strong sense of right and wrong and strives to do the right thing.

Eric is the quintessential Apple/Mac guy. At the core, Apple people frequently see themselves as different from Microsoft/Windows people. Although both systems may be similar in some functions, there seems to be a perceived loyalty and creative advantage that flows from the Apple camp. It's not a moral or ethical issue, but creative people are frequently Apple people. They approach the universe dominated by their right-brain activity while slaves to rules created by left-brain people.

I love, admire and respect Eric, and I thank God that he's my friend for there was a time that our relationship was severely tested and could have failed.

MOTIVE ISSUES

Mac's Apple logo makes you think of creativity. But the apple also has an association with corruption in the Garden of Eden. The problem seems to flow from the truth that we are usually poor judges of our own motives. Eric was formerly the tech intern at our church. He had been trained by the former tech director.

Unfortunately, the former tech director had to leave the church under less-than-ideal circumstances, and this created a hole in the tech ministry. Mixed emotions flowed into my heart like two streams. One stream was clear, and the other muddy, and when they flowed together into one river they were difficult to distinguish because the whole river was now murky. In one stream there was sadness, because the former director was capable, talented, and most importantly, loved God. He made a huge difference in advancing and expanding the ministry of the church. Also, I liked and cared about him. The other stream was characterized by relief. There were some big attitude problems. The former director wasn't an ideal team player, could be self-righteous, and at times had the rest of the staff walking on eggshells. Occasionally, you could cut the tension with a knife.

The former tech director had trained and mentored Eric. Eric's tech gifts were honed, and he also developed a deeper relationship with God. When the training began, Eric was young and impressionable. His mentor had great influence for good, but also created some residual attitudes that were less than ideal. Suffice it to say, the former tech director had a different perspective on some aspects of serving others than the rest of the church staff. These issues were so significant that there had to be a parting of ways. This was an incredibly painful experience for all involved.

Before the actual parting of the ways arrived, the conflicts with the former director became more frequent and intense. His motives for ministry were questioned, and despite repeated meetings there was no change and no resolution. The former director felt that there were no issues with his motives. Essentially he attributed the problems to the other people he worked with. During this time, Eric was indoctrinated into an "us against them" view of ministry where the rest of the staff was perceived as the opposition rather than teammates, family, or community. Clearly, this dynamic was not the Jesus style.

Jesus' motive is to love and serve others. He came to serve, not to be served and to put the needs of others before His own [Mark 10:44-45]. His attitude is so different than our cultural perspective which is essentially selfish and seeks to be served. We are all to have the attitude of Jesus. When we serve others we are to be motivated by love, not a desire to manipulate. For example, when I buy my wife flowers (especially from the florist rather than the guy at the end of the freeway off-ramp), take her to her favorite restaurant, listen attentively to her throughout her favorite meal and dessert, and my plot is motivated by a desire for sex, that is not love and is not service, but is manipulation. Unfortunately all of us, even those in vocational ministry, can lose sight of proper motives for serving others.

When the tech director position became available at the church, Eric was offered the opportunity to step-up into the role. This was a very tenuous time in my relationship with Eric. He was seemingly being torn in two as his heart was pulled in two different directions. He had a sense of allegiance to our church (which I later discovered was more a moral sense of duty than anything else) and at the same time he had a strong emotional and relational connection to his mentor and friend. It was an intense time, and the dynamic was full of confusion about loyalties, motives for ministry, and had all the right ingredients for potential conflict. For the first 30 days I wondered whether Eric was going to quit. If there was going to be restoration of my relationship with Eric, it would be a process (and perhaps a long one). It was as if hundreds of wires had been placed in the wrong connectors, and would need to be slowly and gently removed and reconnected.

Why is it so difficult for most of us to consider our own motives? Generally, when there is a conflict in our relationships we assume that we are right and others are wrong. We tend to judge other people by their actions, but we want others to judge us on our motives. In other words, we want to explain to people *why* we did something. The problem is compounded because we tend to justify our motives as being right. For example, in the midst of the conflict with the tech director, I assumed that my heart was pure, and his was tainted, but I also presume that he felt the same way.

One of the most important questions for us to consider is the following: "Is it me?" To be humble, vulnerable and allow others to honestly assess our motives seems to be difficult for most of us. Our tendency is to attempt to persuade people that we are right and the other person involved in the conflict is wrong. For example, imagine a married couple that is in conflict about spending more time together. He doesn't understand her desires and tells his friends how selfish she is. Meanwhile, she is telling her friends about how selfish he is. Neither one is willing to consider their own selfishness. Unfortunately, most of us won't approach our friends and say, "Where am I blowing it?" It can be uncomfortable to have someone burst your bubble and tell you that your motives, attitudes, and behaviors may not be as pure as you think, but it's necessary.

Why is it so important that our motives are right? Simply stated, when we serve others with the wrong motives it misrepresents God. It is essential that each of us wrestle with the core issues of why we serve others. Let's move beyond the context of the conflict with the former tech director. In other words, put aside any inquiry about who was right or wrong, why the job was offered to Eric, why did he take the job, or what happened to the former director. It seems to Eric and I that Jesus is fundamentally concerned with the issue as to what motivates us to serve. For example, are we serving for approval from people, to feel important or needed, because of guilt, our own satisfaction, or are we genuinely compelled to care for others by our love for God?

MOTIVES **RESTORED**

Eric and I were still at Peet's enjoying coffee, some pastries, and our friendship. We continued to reflect on this earlier chapter in our lives. It had been more than six months since he had become the tech director, and it was the first time that I felt comfortable and secure enough in our relationship to ask Eric what it was like for him at that time. Eric described his own inner struggle and conflict. His mentor had created a sense of suspicion and cynicism in evaluating other people's motives. For example, when one of the other staff members at church affirmed him for doing a good job, his first thought was that they wanted something from him. When someone asked for help he immediately assumed that they were insensitive to how many tasks he was responsible for.

During the first two months Eric was distancing himself from others he worked with. He described his feelings as torment. He was negative, judgmental, and assumed that his motives were right and that others' were wrong. It was a struggle to work with others. But during the second month he discovered that he had misjudged people. He came to appreciate that he actually worked with some good and godly people.

Eric told me about his epiphany experience while reading a T.S. Eliot poem. I had never read any T.S. Eliot poetry. I had no idea what he was talking about so he explained. A section of the poem describes insects being pinned to a display board so that people may observe them. The butterfly is spread out and exposed and people view it and quickly assume they know all there is to know about the butterfly, but really they don't. While the butterfly is pinned to the display it is unable to move its wings and fly. Eric realized that this poem described what was happening in his life. He was doing the same to people as he judged them, without really knowing their story. He was pinning them down and judging their actions and presuming he knew their motives, but really he hadn't stopped to discover their intents. As a result Eric was held back from authentic relationships with others.

Ironically, whenever we pin others we become pinned. When Eric discovered that he may have wrongly judged others, and needed to examine his own motives, he was set free. As Eric and I sat at Peet's, he wondered whether he had grown or if he was still stuck like a butterfly pinned to a display board.

When he started to talk to me about butterflies, the first thought that went into my mind was *metamorphosis*. I assured him that he had grown and that he has been transformed. I was impressed that Eric was able to examine his motives and truly grow through this whole experience. I thought about what Paul wrote, "When I was a child, I spoke as a child, I understood as a child, I thought as a child; but when I became a man I put away childish things." This last year, I watched a young man become spiritually mature. Anytime someone will consider their motives, and honestly examine their lives, it's evidence of spiritual maturity.

It is perplexing to consider that we can do God's work with the wrong motive. I don't mean the scam artists on TV ripping desperate people off in the name of religion, but people who genuinely think they're doing the right thing, people who are unable or unwilling to see any attitude or motive issues. It seems that Jesus was constantly in conflict with the religious leaders of His day, especially the Pharisees, challenging their motives. The Pharisees started off with a seemingly pure motive. They wanted to stay true to God and stay separated from the influence of the world around them. When Alexander the Great conquered the known world about 300 years before Christ, he sought to bring Greek culture into those territories — including Israel. The Greeks were not only the premier military power, but they were recognized as the great philosophers, artists, athletes, mathematicians, physicians, and intellectuals of the ancient world. Rather than try to force Greek culture upon his subjects, Alexander made Greek culture so attractive that most people willingly adopted its culture and religion.

The Pharisees' initial motive was to oppose the spread of Greek culture into the religious and social life of Israel. They developed traditions to maintain the purity of the Jewish faith. They passed these traditions from one generation to the next, but somewhere along the way, God's motives were lost. The problem is that the wrong philosophy, motive or attitude in serving God is passed to others by example. Unfortunately, the Pharisees were convinced that their hearts were pure and Jesus was wrong. They could not honestly consider their motives. Remember, whenever you are arguing with Jesus you're wrong.

The only right motive to serve God and others is love. I don't want to be like the Pharisees. As much as possible I want to be motivated by love for God and others and to represent Jesus well. I'm learning to assume that it is just as likely that I'm wrong as another. We all need to consider whether our attitudes and behaviors reflect Jesus. We need to examine our hearts and be willing to hear from others who may reveal a diagnosis of heart problems. The prescription is to draw closer to Jesus and learn to love people as He does. When motives are wrong we need to ask forgiveness and seek to change – to be transformed like a caterpillar that becomes a butterfly. Remember that if we refuse a heart exam, or refuse to fill the prescription, unfortunately, we will likely infect others with a wrong attitude and motive because we will misrepresent Jesus.

Similarly, there is that old saying about one apple affecting the whole bushel. An apple can look beautiful on the outside, but once you get beneath the skin you can see any damage. When improper motives are discovered we should cut them out of our heart like a bruise on an apple. Then the fruit is available to enjoy. When the fruit at the core is good, the potential of the seed and the apple are revealed. Although it's true that anyone can count the number of seeds in an apple, only God can count the number of apples in a seed. There is great potential when we serve God with the right motives.

CHAPTER TWELVE

PIZZERIA COLISEO

[THE PURSUIT OF PASSION]

PASSIONATE **PURSUIT**

What do you get passionate about? I love pizza. It's probably one of my favorite foods. There are a lot of things I love: my wife, my kids, God, glass bottle Cokes pulled out of an ice chest, the smell and feel of fresh-cut grass, Dodger dogs, perfect cappuccinos, fountain pens, playing drums, puppies ... So when I say, "I love pizza," there must be some nuance you'd like to discern. For example, does this guy obsess so much about pizza that he needs a 12-step program, or does he simply dig pizza like some people like jazz or R&B?

It's not that I like all pizza, and please resist the obvious temptation to label me a "pizza snob" and dismiss all that I want to share with you. You see my parents are New Yorkers and, despite the fact that I was born and raised in California, there is a presumed genetic predisposition toward thinner-crust pizza. My parents, and older brother, too, seemed to like to fold their pizza in the middle. They would begin to consume their pizza while the cheese was still hot enough to pull the skin off your upper palate. I tend to prefer a knife and fork, until I get to the crust which is simply consumed as finger food.

I'm not a big fan of Domino's, although my sons have attempted to persuade me that "it's the best!" Poor misguided souls. It is everything I dislike in a pizza: too "doughy" like a loaf of Wonder bread, tasteless cheese, generic sauce, and it reminds me of the pizza in the school cafeteria. It has all the character and charm of a stick pen ... but that's another story.

At this point, I hope you want to know (perhaps you're even salivating in anticipation, and if not, you will be) what pizzas I like, or shall I say *love*. Well if you must know, I will share with you the seemingly divine destination on the quest for the perfect pizza. Be warned, the tale will experience detours if you're prepared to embark on this journey.

The location is off the beaten path. First, you must journey to Nicaragua, the second poorest country in the Western Hemisphere (a fact you're unlikely to read in your tourist brochure). Once you get to Nicaragua, you'll travel to the capital city, Managua, and from there you begin an ascent through the lush volcanic countryside to the village of Masaya. The town is known for the woodwork craftsmen (and their beautiful handcrafted furniture) who have congregated to the area.

Then, as you travel down the main road, you come to it: Pizzeria Coliseo. As you enter, you feel that you've stepped into a café in Rome. There are murals of the Coliseum painted on the mustard-brown walls and heavy wooden furniture, typical of the village but also presumably of the Mediterranean cafes of Italy. The owner is Fausto, from Rome, and he and his wife ooze hospitality from every pore. Forgive me, we're not here to consider hospitality or ambiance, but to consider what could make this pizza so special that I've now exhausted hundreds of words (about 550 so far) to tell you about it.

When I first bit into Fausto's pizza, (after cutting with knife and fork, for Nicaragua is a civilized country despite its poverty), a rhapsody of flavor exploded from that miniature triangle — a mouthwatering essence that assured me that my quest for the perfect pizza had ended. We had arrived at Shangri La. I continued to consume this delicacy, and when we finished the first, we ordered and finished another pizza.

I began to talk with Fausto, for I had to know his secret. I simply hope and pray that I will not be guilty of divulging a national security treasure as I impart this secret to you. At this point you should be leaning forward to hear the hushed tones I'm about to utter. Fausto gets his mozzarella and his wheat for dough from different regions of the country depending on the rainfall. In essence, the amount of rain in an area will affect the grains such as wheat, as well as the grass the cows will eat that will ultimately yield the milk that will become mozzarella. Furthermore, since there are no hormone issues, FDA monitoring, or other regulations by an agency, there is nothing but unbridled flavor.

I always get so excited when I tell this story. I tend to make big hand gestures, so it is difficult to type right now. My kids have heard me tell the story so many times, that they can do me telling the story better than I do. I'd have them tell you, but alas they're in school getting an education so that their precious lives are not reduced to telling seemingly meaningless pizza stories ... where was I?

Fausto's sauce is a symphony of homegrown spices and tomatoes, the dough is always hand tossed (no cookie cutter cardboard pizza here), thin, and cooked in a wood burning oven. Even my friend Eric, the world traveler, concedes, "That's great pizza!"

Fausto is passionate about making pizza: he loves pizza. I respect and admire that truth. He doesn't talk about being the best, and I presume that he has no aspiration to become the world's biggest pizza establishment. Yet, every year for a period of five years, I have journeyed to experience Fausto's pizza at the pizza Mecca, Pizzeria Coliseo.

At this point, I presume you're pondering the obvious question, "Does he travel all this way just for pizza, even great pizza?" If the answer is affirmative, then perhaps a 12-step program is appropriate. Let me assure you, I'm drawn to Nicaragua for other reasons.

PASSION **TO HELP**

I first went to Nicaragua to support an orphanage and a nearby fledgling church. The church is in the Barrio Santa Ana: one of the poorest neighborhoods, in the poor capital city in the second poorest country in the Western Hemisphere.

My friend Brian was with me. Brian was a deacon at our church. He's young, athletic, good-looking, and an engineer. With Brian the glass is neither half-empty nor half-full; it is simply twice the size of the contents therein. He's truly compassionate and incredibly resourceful — he'll solve almost any problem. His sense of humor is fantastic, but dry like a desert. He's faithful as a St. Bernard. I don't recall Brian really being into pizza, but I presume mountain-bike types generally aren't, so I've never held that against him.

Brian and I began to develop relationships with people in Managua and we found ourselves coming back year after year (not only for pizza). Brian then decided that God was calling him to be a full-time missionary at Calvary Chapel in Managua. Shortly thereafter, Brian found himself serving at this church in a seemingly God-forsaken area. The area is impoverished and hopeless. The primary industry is prostitution; and the drugs of choice are glue-sniffing and homemade alcohol that can cause blindness or even death. The neighborhood is just a few blocks from Lake Managua, and although it sounds romantic, all types of waste pour into the lake. Similarly, a large electrical tower by the lake has hundreds of birds perched upon it, and that would seem to be a lovely sight until you get close enough to discover that they're vultures.

The people of Nicaragua have experienced Communist revolution, Sandinistas, Contras, and every host of "good guy/bad guy" ideology. There is frequently a culture of dependence, whether upon the government or the church. The spiritual temperature is predominantly Catholic, and might be best described as somewhere between indifferent to religious. Essentially, they generally have no interest in God. They may observe religious ritual, but they rarely display any evidence of a desire for a relationship with God.

In the midst of this scene, Brian has faithfully sought to help people grow in their relationship with God. He desires nothing more or nothing less than seeing lives transformed. In essence, he wants to see a true passion for God displayed by the people he serves in Managua. Now after two years, he feels frustrated by the lack of passion. This is apparently a common theme experienced by people who want to mentor and motivate others.

I was having pizza with Jeff, the youth pastor at our church. Our local pizza is pretty good, but you've figured out by now that this story is not really about pizza, but rather about passion. Jeff is a good friend who loves the Lord. He's passionate and excited about everything, a true optimist. If Jeff walked into a room full of manure, he'd probably be happy, 'cause he figures there must be a pony nearby. We all love Jeff, and his enthusiasm is inspiring.

Jeff was bemoaning the struggles of wanting to encourage the youth of our city to be passionate about God. I could sense his pain. When the eternal optimist is sad, you know there must be a good reason. I look at the youth at our church and I'm encouraged because I see a lot of young people who seem to have real zeal for God. Nevertheless, I can't help but connect Brian's and Jeff's struggles, and I presume many other Christian leaders and followers alike. It is a struggle that transcends geographic and cultural boundaries. Brian and Jeff simply want to help people be passionate about God. At times they get frustrated because of the apathy and their inability to create zeal in others.

FINDING **PASSION**

Certainly passion is more than a manifestation of demonstrative behavior, but there will be some evidence in your life that you are passionate about something. What causes some people to be passionate? What causes Fausto to be passionate about pizza? What causes Chicago Cubs fans to love their "Cubbies" despite a century of mediocrity? What causes Chicago Bears fans to remove their shirts and jackets in the dead of a winter blizzard to spell out BEARS across pale, white, barrel-shaped chests (besides alcohol), and what causes Grateful Dead aficionados, affectionately referred to as "Dead Heads," to ignore the facts that it is not the 1960s and Jerry Garcia has left the auditorium?

I wish I knew why some people are passionate about God. I'm not sure that I fully know the motivation, but I do recognize passion when I see it. I heard a story once that I think may be illuminating. The story involves a jeweler named Harry Winston. One day a very wealthy man came into Harry's store. He was looking at a very rare and expensive diamond. The salesman knew all about diamonds; from a technical standpoint he was outstanding. He could answer any question, and provide all the information about diamonds. After awhile, the wealthy man prepared to leave. That's when Harry interceded and began to show the diamond one more time.

This time, the man purchased the diamond from Harry. He wondered, "Why did I buy the diamond from you, when I was prepared to leave after the other man showed me the same diamond?" Harry explained, "He knows more about diamonds than anyone I know, maybe even more than me, but I love them!" In essence, it was Harry's love for diamonds that was contagious. His love stirred passion in himself and others.

Through the years, I've discovered some ways that don't work, that don't create passion. For example, guilt is not an ideal means to create passion. For some reason, telling me that I'm bad and blowing it, because I'm apathetic toward God, just doesn't seem to stir me for too long. I presume that there is a time for scolding, but guilt is not the essence of an ideal relationship.

For example, I could try to motivate my kids to visit an older relative by telling them it's the right thing to do and if they don't want to, they're selfish. Inevitably, they will say, "Do we have to?"

And Karen and I will reply, "No you *get to*!" The essence of this motivation style is guilt. Parents establish what is right, and then urge kids that it's wrong (and thus they're guilty) for not *wanting* to do what's right. Church leaders who try to motivate primarily by guilt are unlikely to create an ideal relationship with God.

Similarly, trying to create excitement doesn't seem to generate long-lasting passion either. Don't get me wrong, I love a parade, dog-and-pony show, or sporting event as much as the next guy. Unfortunately, in and of themselves, they fail to instill lasting change, zeal or passion. Too often church leaders try to motivate primarily by drawing people to an exciting event.

Getting back to the example of the kids visiting an older relative, imagine the parents motivating the kids to visit grandma because she has the newest game system and the game they've been begging to play. It's not too difficult to imagine that it would be pretty easy to get the kids packed up in the car to see grandma. Unfortunately, the thrill will fade all too quickly. Even if grandma keeps upgrading the game system and continues to provide the most popular games the motivation won't last. The kids weren't drawn to grandma but to entertainment, and the availability of alternative entertainment will soon eliminate a willingness or desire to see grandma.

My aunt is now 92 years old. She has survived her four siblings, including her youngest sister, my mom. In her bedroom is a large sepia-tone photograph. The picture shows my aunt and her new husband, and my grandfather and grandmother walking down the Boardwalk in Atlantic City, New Jersey. The Boardwalk is full of pedestrian traffic, and there are very few cars in the background of this image captured in the 1930s. All of the women in the picture have long dresses, and all the men have suits and hats. The image captures a moment in time as they walk on the Boardwalk by the beach. It is one of my favorite photos.

The photo became a springboard for my kids to connect with their great aunt and her life. As they asked questions about the picture and about her world, they discovered someone who was interesting to them and a life that was different than their own. As she asked about their lives they, too, wanted to share. It was by sharing their experiences and their hearts that they became connected.

People become passionate about God when they begin to understand Him and learn how interesting a life in God is. Passion can't be created by guilt or maintained by entertainment. Instead, it is a result of relationship – by drawing close. When I discover what God has done for me, the unconditional and unmerited love that He has shown me, it is only reasonable for me to want to love Him back. When I'm in Him, I'm excited to be there. Interestingly, our English word "enthusiasm" comes from the Greek *en Theos* meaning "in God."

PASSION **PERIL**

Why is passion for God necessary? Everyone is passionate about something or someone in their life. Each of us has a master desire. For some it is: their career, education, power, possessions, position, recreation or relationship(s). In effect, whatever is your master passion is the object of desire – or worship. It has become your god.

The Bible explains that we shall become like the object of our passion. If you idolize an athlete, singer/songwriter, or actor, you will seek to develop attributes like them. If wealth is your master passion then the accumulation of wealth and possessions will be your focus. Those of us who are particularly selfish have tended to make ourselves the object of our worship. Unfortunately, a person who is all wrapped up in themselves is a very small package.

Despite shortcomings with the church as an institution, there are many healthy churches that effectively help people grow in their relationship with Jesus. The more I learn about Jesus, the more I want to be like Him. As I discover the real Jesus, there is a genuine love that fuels passion. The passion tends to be life-transforming. I've found that people who are in love with Jesus tend to develop Christ-like characteristics: love, joy, peace, kindness, goodness, gentleness, faithfulness, patience, and self-control. I can't imagine why anyone would not want to be like Jesus.

My healthiest relationships have been fostered simply by spending time and sharing my heart with another and learning about them. Similarly, I learn about God by reading the Bible, prayer, and discovering what God is revealing about Himself to others. Someone who models a genuine passion for God has also often been helpful to me. That's my encouragement to Brian, Jeff, you and me. Their example of an intimate relationship with God is an effective lesson. Brian and Jeff are both solid Bible teachers, but sometimes great truths are caught rather than taught. People will see a genuine love for God demonstrated by someone's behaviors and attitudes perhaps even more than what they proclaim or say.

My pastor, Chuck Smith, has never been one to try to manipulate people, make them feel guilty, or try to ride a wave of emotional excitement as a means to generate passion. I love Chuck for countless reasons, not the least of which has been his unwavering example during my entire Christian life. Pastor Chuck is a tremendous Bible teacher who simply communicates simple truth simply. He doesn't rely upon dramatic or theatrical oratory, but simply helps us to understand God and the Bible, and to learn how to apply those truths to our lives. One of the many lessons that he has communicated to me, and countless others who have been influenced by his life, is this profound perspective: focus on what God has done for people rather than what they can do for God. As we discover God's love for us and His greatness, it is reasonable to be passionate in our love for God.

Passion flows from love. Love flows from understanding and connection. Fausto loves pizza, Harry loves diamonds, and Brian and Jeff love Jesus. When you really love something or someone, you want everyone else to experience that feeling, and share that love. Passion can't be contained — it erupts from your very being like red-hot lava flows from a volcano. Thus, others see or soon discover what we're really passionate about.

We are all passionate about something or someone. What do you get passionate about? If we only get passionate about pizza, helping others, sports, music or anything else besides God, we'll miss out on becoming all that we could be. We'll miss out on being like Jesus, and that's the greatest peril of not being passionate about Him.

CHAPTER THIRTEEN

ONE

[THE BEAUTY OF WORSHIP
BEFORE AN AUDIENCE OF ONE]

DESIRE **TO BE NUMBER ONE**

I hate it when the desire for affirmation, mine or anyone else's, obscures God. I was talking to my friend Ed the other day about the blessings and burdens of ministry. Ed is a very humble pastor and we only get to see each other one to two times a year since we live so far apart from one another. I asked, "So Ed, what's been the hardest part of ministry the last year?" He replied, "It's been tough with J.J. I had to ask him to step down from ministry." I'm sure my face contorted but I'm not sure what the expressions were saying. What I was feeling was a bit of surprise, not shock, and a great deal of sadness and disappointment. I stared into my coffee cup and quickly reflected.

I had met J.J. the year before. He is a young man who desires to be a pastor. He is tall, thin, good looking, has a great smile, and he can sing. J.J. has so much potential as a leader. When he leads worship at the church, he sings not only beautifully but passionately and the church follows his lead. I looked up from my coffee, and weakly asked, "What happened?" Ed's reply was simple, too simple, just one word: "Pride." I said, "What do you mean? Elaborate." He looked across the table, first at me, then at Tom, then at Justin. Ed said, "Justin close your ears. It seems that every worship leader struggles with pride." Justin, is the lead worshiper at our church, and he quickly agreed, "Amen."

J.J. struggled with the passion for position, prominence, and perhaps power and pleasure. J.J.'s yearning for affirmation and approval from people, and the desire to feel better than, and more important than, someone, anyone, or possibly everyone, is a dangerous condition. Unfortunately it is a plague that infects so much of mankind. Instead of seeking to please an audience of One, J.J. desired to be number one, and that longing was his undoing. It brought him down and made him less effective as he sought to serve God. I was grieved, and began to reflect. Why does this happen?

PROBLEM **OF PRIDE**

The pride problem and the passion struggle unfortunately are not new. It has played out since before time as we know it. In God's story, the prophets Isaiah and Ezekiel describe the problem of pride and the fall of the first worship leader [Isaiah 14:12-15, Ezekiel 28:1-20]. Lucifer was the worship leader of heaven, but in his pride, he wanted to be number one. Essentially, from Lucifer's position, there was only one higher rung on the corporate ladder – God Himself. Lucifer in his pride wanted God's position and is swiftly removed by God from ministry and is cast out from heaven. He then becomes man's adversary – Satan.

The story reveals that as Lucifer served as heaven's worship leader; he received praise and attention for the beautiful gifts that were manifest in and through him. Although Lucifer was a magnificent created being, he was nonetheless a created being. Therefore, by seeking and desiring praise, Lucifer obscured God. All of God's creation should bring glory to God. The sun, moon and stars bring glory to God. The earth's beautiful waterfalls, flowers, rainbows, and animals cooperate in God's plan without reservation. It is only man (and angels) that struggles in this conflict: the struggle between pride and giving glory to God.

Every person who has influence will encounter this struggle. Regardless of whether you serve at a church, stand on a platform, or are engaged in any one of the countless roles in the marketplace or in life in general. When people recognize the God-given gifts and abilities that are displayed in you and by you, they will tend to praise you. There will be a potential temptation to want to receive glory rather than direct the glory to God or give Him the credit. This struggle must be fascinating from God's perspective. When a worship leader fails to direct people to God, it must be particularly ugly to God. The very people who should help others to see God can get in the way.

Each of us has a desire for affirmation and attraction. For some the need seems to be insatiable. That desire for approval can create a conflict in a relationship with God. As people who want to be like Jesus, we should want to direct praise and attention to God rather than seeking affirmation for self. Therefore, each of us must work through this conflict and seek to direct people to praise God. How can we discover a proper way to handle our desire for affirmation or approval from others?

HUMBLE **HEARTS**

In contrast to J.J. there is Justin or J.B., the lead worshiper at our church. As I looked at him, as he sat at the table with Ed, Tom and I, I truly appreciated his desire to cultivate a humble heart. Justin is like a son to me. He is just 20 years old, but God has given him wisdom beyond his years. He is fun, has a great sense of humor, and is deep. He loves music and loves to read books about God and the Christian life as well as great classic literature. He writes his experiences and feelings in a journal and writes songs to express them. He has the rare ability to pull off wearing almost any item of clothing. His blond hair has seemingly been worn in countless styles.

Before he became a worship leader, he was a talented musician. He plays guitar, drums and saxophone. He has diverse music tastes and played rock, alternative and jazz. He played clubs and all sorts of gigs but was never fulfilled despite the size of the audience.

Justin then began to play guitar as part of a worship team for the youth group at another church. He began to experience a greater sense of satisfaction playing worship music than playing before any other audience. He was becoming a worshiper rather than merely a musician.

Justin started to come to the same church as me, and got

involved with the church's youth group. He was initially mentored by Gary, the former youth pastor at the church. Gary is also like a son to me. He is a great Bible teacher, a man who loves to learn. He is full of wisdom yet remains humble. A humble heart does not seek to be the center of attention, directs praise to God, and seeks to avoid obscuring God. Of all the many statements that Jesus made in the New Testament, there is only one autobiographical statement. Jesus said that He was humble [Matthew 11:28-29].

After a couple of years, Justin became an intern at the church. He continued to grow as a worshiper and as a young man. He was developing a heart for God and a humble heart. Then the opportunity arose for a church staff position, and to become the lead worshiper at our church. The opportunity and the responsibility are significant. There are five different worship teams at our church and they lead the congregation in praising God. Although Justin is overseeing people who are older than he is, they all appear to respect and support his leadership. Overseeing the worship ministry of a church is a great responsibility. The opportunity is also tremendous, a dream come true for a young worship leader. Leading worship at a large growing church can be a coveted position. During this season, I have the privilege of knowing Justin, and helping to mentor him along his journey with God.

Standing on a platform in a church and representing God in front of a crowd of people can be one of the most precarious places imaginable. It is truly a privilege to represent God before people but most of us who have stood on the platform know how dangerous it can be. It's not a physical danger of falling off an elevated stage, but the danger of seeking praise from people. Affirmation and "applause" from people can be intoxicating and seductive – I know from experience.

Where there is seduction, there is danger, like the beautiful song of the sirens that sent ships crashing to destruction. In Homer's epic, *The Odyssey*, Ulysses ultimately sails safely past. With careful foresight he heeded the warnings and placed beeswax in the ears of all the sailors so they could not be seduced by the song. Yet, Ulysses is so enraptured, so curious, so seduced, that he orders his sailors to safely tie him to the ship's mast so that he will be able to hear the song, but unable to grab the rudder and crash the ship.

That's how it can be on the platform. Pastors, musicians, and singers are all supposed to be there to help people see God ... to lead others into worship. Anyone on the platform who has acquired any level of spiritual maturity, any depth of soul, abhors the thought of entertaining or performing at church. To reduce worship and intimacy with God to a show is one of the ugliest thoughts I can wrestle with, and I can't even begin to imagine what it looks like from God's perspective.

Therefore, we begin to fear the praise and affirmation of people, like the beautiful song of the sirens. If we start to listen, and let the praise of people resonate against our ego, we turn our ear to them, rather than turning our eyes to Him. We turn the rudder toward the voice of the sirens to hear more of their beautiful song. Perhaps ever so slowly, we change course to enhance the praise and affirmation of people. Slowly, almost imperceptibly drawn through the shroud of the fog of compliments, we drift away from true worship until we crash against the jagged rocks. There we discover many other vessels destroyed by the song of the sirens.

In *The Odyssey*, Ulysses realized the danger and took measures to avoid crashing his ship and injuring those entrusted to his care. He was sober and wise. Although he carefully protected the other sailors from hearing, Ulysses could not bear the idea of not hearing the siren's song for himself. He was tempted and felt that he *needed* to hear the song. Even epic heroes are flawed, and the desires of their flesh can be just as dangerous to themselves and others, as the motives of other mortals.

So, wise spiritual leaders, those who realize the danger of the platform, warn themselves and others of the danger. They try to make sure that everyone has beeswax in their ears so that they can stay on course. They genuinely seek to focus on worship before an audience of One. Alas, leading worship is an epic struggle. Those who have been gifted by God with a talent to sing, to make an instrument sing, or to communicate with the voice of an angel, will undoubtedly hear praise from people. Like Ulysses, we have sought to tie ourselves to the mast, away from the rudder, so that we cannot crash the vessel. But, we are reluctant to stuff our ears with wax. The need for affirmation and our insecurities are satiated by their kind and encouraging words ... so beautiful, so seductive.

We learn quickly to deflect the glory with trite and appropriate clichés, "Praise God" and, "Thanks for the kind encouragement." Those efforts are noble and good, like being tied to a mast. Yet, to the extent that the words are *needed* to satisfy, there is still danger. It can be so subtle: the problem of pride and the desire for a humble heart. For example, we have multiple services at our church. After the first service, I'll ask the pastors at our church, "What needs to change before the second service?" In that case, I'm asking what changes need to be made to the service or the teaching to improve and prepare for the next service. Somewhat akin to a coach at halftime trying to make adjustments before the team goes out for the rest of the game. In contrast, I can ask my wife the seemingly innocuous question, "What did you think of church today?" The question seems pure and innocent enough, but can be loaded with an egocentric inquiry. In other words, I may be essentially asking, "How was *my* message?" Again, the danger of looking for affirmation from people rather than from God is exposed.

God instructed His people in the Old Testament that those who served in the temple must have attained a certain chronological age (30); in the New Testament the emphasis is spiritual maturity rather than chronology. In either case, it appears the reason is the same:

to ensure a sufficient level of emotional and spiritual maturity that those representing God can recognize the problem of pride and can navigate toward a humble heart without crashing the vessel in the process.

The ones who are developing a humble heart recognize that truly it's all about God and helping people to see Him. In essence, the humble become invisible and merely direct people to Him. John the Baptist understood this when he declared, "He must increase, but I must decrease" [John3:30]. Developing that type of spiritual maturity is a lifelong process. The leaders who frighten me the most are the ones who are totally ignorant of the danger, or think that they have overcome so that they are no longer at risk. The leaders who tend to inspire me are aware of the conflict and desire to continually develop a humble heart. But, how do we develop a humble heart?

BEAUTY **OF WORSHIP**

My friend Robb is a pastor and a worship leader at our church. I love talking with Robb (and sharing my stories with him) because he's a thinker. He's deep and likes to ponder. He loves to reflect upon God. Robb is a proficient singer and musician, but more importantly he has soul … he loves to worship God. Robb has been leading worship for about 20 years and has gleaned plenty of wisdom. He appreciates and struggles with many of the complicated issues about leading worship. For example, can the church audience's expectation for excellent musicians and vocalists pressure a worship leader to disqualify a less talented worshiper in favor of a technically more proficient person who lacks a heart to worship God? Can better quality musicians and singers help facilitate worship of God, or is an assembly merely enraptured with talented people? Is there a healthy godly sense of "pride" that seeks excellence for God's glory? How can people meet their desire for affirmation in a healthy way? Robb understands some of the challenges of a lead worshiper's desire to focus and worship God and the potential distraction of simultaneously leading a worship team as well as the congregation. Robb simply desires to experience the beauty of worship and help others to do the same.

Justin lacks Robb's experience but shares a similar heart, mind and soul. Despite his youth, Justin inspires me to worship. He has discovered the danger of seeking praise from people, and the beauty of worship before an audience of One. It is not that he has arrived such that he no longer is tempted by affirmation, but the fact that he is aware of the struggle encourages me. He recognizes the angst of the struggle, and writes about it with passion. The feelings are set to his music and appear inspired by God. Sometimes when a worship leader tells me, "God just gave me this song ..." I might think, "Don't blame that on God" or "Ask Him to take it back." On the other hand, it seems that God has truly given Justin some songs, as J.B. humbly sought God.

Justin wrote a song called *Life Worth Living*. It's a beautiful expression of worship and one of my favorite songs. I love all the verses, as well as this chorus :

You've opened my eyes, You set me free
You gave me life worth living
I bow, here at Your feet asking You please
Jesus make me like You

J.B. and I were eating sushi after church recently and I asked about the inspiration for the song. J.B. explained that it's autobiographical. He had just returned from a mission trip to Ukraine and was seeking direction for his life. He was considering Bible College, working at our church, and other options. He came to the realization that all of us are proud. Some of us are ignorant of that fact, and some are truly seeking humility. All of us have been prodigal sons and daughters. We don't have to go to Las Vegas or chase the ultimate party. We all tend to seek pleasure from the things of the world rather than the things of God. He had discovered that we all need to humble ourselves before God, declare our dependence upon him, and learn to seek less attention for ourselves. In between bites of sushi, J.B. shared his thoughts, "It's all about God's grace. He gives us a life worth living ... to enjoy God. It's not about our efforts and our accomplishments, but it's all about Him."

I reflected on the desire for affirmation, the problem of obscuring God, and a potential solution. We develop a humble heart by seeking God and discovering His great love for us. A life worth living is founded in knowing God and *His* love for us, not affirmation from people. The yearning for approval from people only leads to striving, frustration and bitterness. The closer we draw to Jesus, the less affirmation and attention we need from people. It becomes progressively easier to direct praise to God rather than seeking it for self. Worship before an audience of One is not merely singing praise songs to God, but is a life devoted to receiving God's love and then living for His approval more than the approval of other people. When we choose a life worth living, we are less likely to obscure God and far more likely to reveal Jesus to others. May J.J., my other friends, as well as you and I choose to worship before an audience of One.

CHAPTER FOURTEEN

THE REAL JESUS

[CAN THE REAL JESUS
BE FOUND AMONG "RELIGIOSITY?"]

WHAT IS JESUS LIKE?

Have you ever wanted to find the real Jesus, and felt frustrated by the case of mistaken identity? Can the real Jesus be found among the impostors and all the "religiosity" that creates confusion?

When I try to imagine what Jesus is like, it is difficult to overcome the cultural iconic Jesus. Typically, He's depicted as a Caucasian, albeit well-tanned, with shoulder-length brown hair. He's thin and muscular, and has an ankle-length robe. He has a neatly trimmed beard. He seems to walk everywhere with a lamb around His neck. He has a gentle smile and perfect white teeth. Today, I'd imagine Jesus wearing jeans, T-shirt, sandals and a leather WWID? bracelet [What Would I Do?].

The Bible says that He wasn't physically remarkable. He had no physical beauty that made Him particularly desirable. There was nothing about His looks that made Him stand out from the crowd. When Judas betrayed Him, he told the religious leaders, "It is the One that I kiss." In other words, Judas had to identify Him because He looked like everybody else. Judas didn't say, "It's the guy with the glowing head."

It's important to see that Jesus can fit into your life. I imagine Jesus hanging out at Peet's Coffee. He'd dig cappuccinos and rarely order decaf. He'd write with a fountain pen into a cool journal and would likely use brown ink. Jesus would invite me to sit at His table and I'd ask Him what He was writing. As He shows me the pages, I'm overwhelmed by the depth of His thoughts: the angst, the passion, and the intellectual insight. Yet, He walks me through the pages to ensure that I understand. I even marvel at His sketches and drawings.

I believe that whatever you're into, Jesus will meet you there. If you're a guy who likes to work in the workshop, Jesus will meet you there (remember, He is a carpenter). If you're into raising a family, so is Jesus. Even though He was never married and had no kids, He is definitely the expert, and He gives great advice on the subject throughout the Bible. I'm confident that the real Jesus would love to help strengthen my marriage and family, and would talk with me and guide me through my family issues. When I consider what the real Jesus is like, I think first of all that He'll meet me in the context of my life. But that is not a complete picture of the real Jesus.

Sometimes when I think of what Jesus is like, I often think of some of the people that have expressed the heart of Jesus. My friend Kristina was with me on a trip to Nairobi. We were in Kibera, the world's largest, most densely populated slum; more than one million people solidly packed into a shanty town only one mile by three miles. She cried as she contemplated that intense poverty and hardship. She realized that the problem is not assets, but our allocation of them. People are always trying to push ahead. She fought back tears and declared, "There'd be no traffic and no poverty if we weren't so busy trying to get ahead of one another and constantly pushing others out of the way!" I recognized the heart of Jesus in her words.

There are only a few people that I've met that left a distinct impression upon me that I had been in the presence of Jesus. The first one was Ethylene. She was living at an assisted-living residence in Southern California. It was a large center with about 100 apartments, and a big community center. I had contacted the director of the center about doing a Bible study for the senior residents, and we scheduled a meeting at the center. When I arrived, one of the residents, Ethylene, approached me. She was petite with shiny white hair. She wore a large rhinestone broach, about the size of a billboard that spelled JESUS. She asked why I was there and I replied, "I'm hoping to start a Bible study for the residents." Ethylene placed my hand between hers, looked deep into my eyes, and said, "Darling, you are an answer to my prayers."

Ethylene shined like a bright light. She demonstrated the faith of God. Despite her advanced years, the presence of God shining forth from her was illuminating. About a year later, I introduced my mother to Ethylene. "Ethylene" I said, "This is my mom, Penny." Ethylene held my mother's hand, as she had held mine about a year before, and said to my mom, "Penny isn't Jesus good!" I interjected, "Ethylene, my mom doesn't know the Lord yet." Ethylene gently patted my mother's hand and said, "Honey, you just don't know what you're missing."

A few weeks later, Ethylene told me that the Lord had spoken to her that she would not die before my mother came to know Jesus. Later, my mom did in fact come to know Jesus as her Lord and Savior. Within the month, Ethylene left this earth to spend eternity with Jesus whom she loved so much. Ethylene reflected Jesus in such a profound way that I wondered, "Is this what Jesus looks like?" I hadn't expected Him to look like an elderly white-haired woman with a rhinestone I.D. badge but perhaps, in some sense, it was Him.

Another was Maggie. I first met her at a woman's refugee center in Nairobi, Kenya. Love flows from every pore of her body. She is round-faced, with a smile that radiates God's love. She walks with a cane, but will make sure that she either gets to you, or you walk her way to receive a warm hug. I asked her, "Maggie, what's your story?" She looked across the table and began to tell me about her journey. About a decade before, she was in a very serious car accident. Every other passenger in the vehicle died. Maggie sustained serious injuries to her leg, which required a hip plate. She now needs the help of a cane to walk. She had been a nurse, but as a result of the accident, she could no longer care for patients. Maggie is so compassionate it was no surprise that she had been a nurse.

Maggie explained that after the accident she was angry at God, and felt discouraged and depressed. Her friend invited her to visit

the woman's refugee center, Amani Ya Juu [Peace of God]. The
women who live at the center have suffered from civil war in
neighboring countries in East Africa. They have lost husbands,
frequently lost children, and many had been beaten and raped.
Maggie said that when she came to the center, she observed the
joy and love these women demonstrated because of their
relationship with Christ.

Maggie was offered an opportunity to work at the center and
share her compassion with them. The women are a community, and
as a family there is a strong bond of love between them. Maggie
told me most ladies stay at the center about four years. I asked,
"How do you feel when they leave?" She began to cry, and then she
explained that it is bittersweet. The women grow in Christ, receive
healing, and they become a family. Then, it is hard to watch them
leave, but she knows that it is time for them to leave the nest. "Are
you still angry at God?" I asked. She said, "No I thank God now.
Had it not been for my accident, I never would have come here and
known God's love the way I know it now."

Every time I'm with Maggie, I sense the presence of God as if
I was standing right before Jesus. I asked her, "Do you have any
questions for me?" She replied, "Before I ask a question, I want to
express thanksgiving that you come from so far away to encourage
me and to share God's love. My only question is, when will you
move here to stay?" For Maggie, it seems to be all about
relationship. There is something about Maggie's countenance that
radiates Jesus. I had never imagined Jesus as a round-faced,
dark-skinned, woman but perhaps, in some sense, it was Him.

Another person who looks like Jesus to me is Don. He is one
of the pastors at our church. He has a mustache and goatee, light
skin, closely shaved hair, and receding hairline; not the stereotypical
image of Jesus. Yet, Don looks like Jesus to me. Don is one of the
kindest people I know.

Don surfs and oversees the men's ministry of the church, but he is not a "macho man." He's plenty tough enough, but his style is gentle. Don always has time for people. He genuinely loves them, cares for them. He seems to me to be a loving shepherd who looks upon people as a good shepherd looks at his sheep. Don seems to care more about relationship than task.

I've never heard Don say anything negative about anyone. He doesn't gossip, doesn't talk about people behind their backs unless he says something positive, and seems to always see the best in people. I marvel at Don, because he won't say something negative even about people who treated him very poorly. Sooner or later, if you spend enough time with people, you'll find out what is really in their heart, because ultimately we will speak what we *really* think. Don has the heart of Jesus. He tends to see the potential in people, and assumes that with enough love, time, and influence, they will progress toward their potential. I never imagined Jesus as a surfer white guy with a receding hairline but perhaps, in some sense, it was Him.

All these people have helped me to see the real Jesus, but that's not all that He is.

WHY IS HE HARD TO FIND?

Why is it so hard to find the real Jesus? I was talking at dinner with Tom, J.B., Burt, Shirley, Kristina, Ed and Kelli, and I asked their take on the issue. We had been talking about the real Jesus as we ate with a view of the lake and the setting sun in the distance. As the question shifted to why is He hard to find, the sun was setting and darkness filled the landscape. It seemed so appropriate. Many good insights were offered by "the family" that sat around the table.

First, we've created God in our own image. Rather than looking to the Bible to discover Jesus, many simply create Jesus with the attributes they want Him to have. They pick and choose characteristics with the same ease and capriciousness as someone at a buffet. Unfortunately, the result is not the real Jesus.

Second, people are often seeking material solutions rather than spiritual. In this approach, Jesus is reduced to a genie in the bottle. People call on Jesus to cater to their desires for prosperity or material gain. We all agreed this type of prosperity teaching misrepresents Jesus. It creates the wrong expectations. Surely, Jesus is concerned about our physical needs, but the priority appears to be spiritual.

Ironically, a major obstacle to seeing the real Jesus is religion. Religious leaders in Jesus' day, up to the present and continuing, are threatened by the real Jesus because He upsets the status quo. Churches frequently misrepresent Jesus by essentially seeking to draw people to a church rather than to Jesus. In addition, churches have contributed to the perception that they simply want money from people and use "religiosity" to extort it. The money issue becomes even more confused by the impostors who merely use religion as a means to scam and deceive the unwitting.

Churches may also inadvertently veil the real Jesus. For example, by emphasizing the "Do's and Don'ts" of religion, we run the risk of reducing Jesus to a mere list of rules. Similarly, the tendency of emphasizing what we must do rather than what He has done obscures the real Jesus. The message of the Bible emphasizes God's love and what He has done for us, not what we must do. However, despite any shortcomings, we all agreed the "local church" has tremendous capacity to introduce people to the real Jesus.

The biggest obstacle is not the church, but a perception that Jesus is not relevant in our modern world. That misperception is compounded by a misunderstanding of who Jesus really is. Alas, the night had grown long, and my friends and I were tired. It was time for bed.

WHO **IS HE?**

The sun was rising over the hills and the lake became visible before us. My friends and I drank tea and coffee, bathing in the silent beauty of a new morning. At breakfast we continued our discussion. I said to my friends, "In the middle of Matthew's gospel, Jesus asked the disciples, 'Who do men say that I, the Son of Man, am?' [Matthew 16:13] It seems to me that Jesus wanted to know what the word on the street was. Who (or what) do you guys think people in *our* culture think Jesus is?" My friends did not hesitate before responding. Many of the replies will sound familiar to you: a rabbi, a philosopher, a wise sage, a man who went around doing good, and a good teacher. "Slow down!" I begged, "I'm trying to write all this down."

"What else?" They eagerly continued: one of many ways to God, a prophet, an example of a good person, an enlightened man. Their replies were likely an accurate reflection of our culture, and were definitely thought-provoking. Two of the most provocative were: a crutch for the weak and a metaphor (i.e., that the events of the Bible are merely folklore, fairytales or myths).

Perhaps, you've wondered who He is and had similar ideas. Jesus wants us to wrestle with the question of His identity and come to the correct conclusion. Not merely as an intellectual concept, but on a very personal level. So Jesus asked His disciples, "But who do you say that I am?" Each person has to decide who Jesus is. There is no more significant issue in our lives than correctly identifying who Jesus really is. If we misidentify Him and see Jesus merely as another person, albeit with great wisdom, we are unlikely to follow Him and yield our lives to God.

Our understanding of who Jesus is will determine our understanding of God. That's why God wants us all to meet and know the real Jesus. Therefore, Jesus makes it a critical issue for each of us as individuals – who do *you* believe Jesus is?

HOW **WILL I KNOW HIM?**

Later, we were gathered around the fireplace. As we stared at the flames, I tossed out another question to my friends, "What would you say to someone who asked, 'How will I know the real Jesus?'" The first reply was to be expected, "You won't have to question – you'll know." "Sure" I said, "But there's got to be something more!" My friends and I then started to wrestle with the question, and then they offered some great insights. J.B. shared, "You want to change. You want to change everything to be like Him." We all agreed, "That's good."

Ed and Burt focused on the feeling of peace, "You have peace *with* God, so you experience the peace *of* God." I agreed, but also wondered if that was just too subjective. Tom had an interesting perspective, "You want to know Him more and more. It's like artichokes; you just want to keep peeling away layers." "Brilliant insight!" I chimed in (perhaps influenced by my fondness for artichokes ... but that's another story). The fire was stoked, the warmth felt comforting, and the glow was mesmerizing.

Then my friends asked what I thought. "Remember when John the Baptist wanted to confirm that Jesus really was the Messiah?" John had come to a crisis in faith [Matthew 11:1-6]. John was in prison, and apparently assumed that if Jesus was really the Messiah that he would have been set free. In other words, his expectations weren't being met. So John sent two of his followers to confirm His identity. Jesus answered John's messengers, "Go and tell John the things which you hear and see: the blind see and the lame walk; the lepers are cleansed and the deaf hear; the dead are raised up and the poor have the gospel proclaimed to them."

Jesus was confirming that He was the Christ by His words and deeds that fulfilled the Old Testament prophecies concerning the Messiah. There are more than 100 prophecies in the Old Testament that relate specifically to the identity of the Messiah. God wanted us to be able to make a positive I.D. of the Christ so that we can be certain that we have found the real Jesus and not an impostor. Essentially, it is statistically impossible for anyone besides Jesus to be the Messiah. When we actually examine the prophecies of the Old Testament and the New Testament record of Jesus' life, death, and resurrection, we see Jesus fulfilling these prophecies. We are faced with evidence beyond a reasonable doubt that Jesus is the Messiah.

Even after the resurrection, Jesus sought to confirm His identity through the Scriptures. Luke's gospel records Jesus' interaction with two disciples on the road to Emmaus, near Jerusalem, shortly after the resurrection [Luke 24:13-32]. They did not yet know that Jesus had risen, and were incredibly sad. As Jesus encountered them, at first they did not recognize Him. Jesus could have confirmed His identity by simply revealing the pierce marks, like He did with Thomas [John 20:26-29], but He chose not to. Instead, beginning in the books of Moses, and all the Prophets, He explained to them in all the Scriptures the things concerning Himself. As Jesus, so to speak, opened the Bible to them, they realized that Jesus' life, death, and resurrection were all true, just like God had predicted in the Bible.

We all agreed that the best way to know the real Jesus is to meet Him through the Bible – through His story. One reason that Jesus came to earth was to reveal God to us so that we could understand Him. We can test any philosophy, belief system, or religion by examining the claims compared to the real Jesus revealed in the Bible. The Bible is a story that introduces us to the True and Living God so that we can know Him and make Him known.

The real Jesus, who we see in the Bible, is amazing and awesome. He is all man and yet, all God. Jesus represents all that God is to us. When you experience Jesus, you've experienced the True and Living God [John 14:7-9]. Our words could never reveal all that God is, because He is infinite, and we are finite. Yet, He has revealed Himself to man through nature, through relationship, the Prophets/Old Testament, and now, most clearly, through Jesus.

The real Jesus demonstrates the depth, height, and length of God's love for us. The Bible reveals God's perfection and holiness. God's nature is so perfect that nothing "imperfect" can enter His presence without being consumed. This is the great dilemma. God created us to have relationship with Him, but our rebellion against God [sin] separates us from God. God is merciful and loving, but He is also entirely just. Therefore, the penalty for sin – death — can't be ignored. Jesus demonstrates the love of God in that He came to this world not only to relate to us, but to pay the penalty for our sin with His life. Thus, whoever wants to have a relationship with God through Jesus can come and God will not reject them [John 3:16]. Jesus is not one of many ways to God, but He declared that He was the only way to God [John 14:6]. Therefore, He is either a very horrible and bad man, a lunatic, or His claim is true.

Jesus is always relevant, because God is always relevant. In a modern world, and a post-modern world, Jesus remains at the epicenter because He is the author and the finisher of a life worth living. Our culture's declaration of independence from God is simply the ages old theme that ushered in the first rebellion – the desire to make ourselves god. Yet, the futility and the vanity of trying to eliminate or ignore God is exposed. Ultimately, man discovers that life without God is *not* a life worth living.

Therefore, we are restless, seeking to find the truth that will bring hope, satisfaction, love, and peace. In our quest, we want assurance that we have found the solution — the real Jesus. So God wants us to be comforted that we can and we will know Him. Ultimately, you choose to believe Him based on the evidence and a step of faith. You simply decide to ask Him into your life, and choose to follow Him rather than your own will. The Bible says that when you do that, God begins an authentic relationship with you and you will begin to be transformed [Acts 16:31]. As you get to know the real Jesus you find yourself loving God more, freeing you up to loving others more. Jesus said that our love would be the test of whether you really know Him [John 13:35, Galatians 5:22-23].

And so we sat cozy around a fireplace secure and comforted that we have found the real Jesus, and confident that you can, too. We may see Him in those who know Him themselves like Kristina, Ethylene, Maggie or Don. And we can surely see Him in the Bible. Our desire to be transformed, to be more like Jesus, and our growing love for God and others assured us that we know Him. Knowing the real Jesus makes all the difference and makes life worth living.

CHAPTER FIFTEEN

STORY

[EVERYONE HAS A STORY
AND SO DOES GOD]

IN THE BEGINNING

Everyone has a story, and so does God. Why do we love good stories? What if God wanted to draw us closer through stories, would you want to explore the idea? The story is God's most complete form of truth-telling. It seems that we connect with stories because God designed us to. Stories help us so that we can connect with Him. I'd love to encourage you to consider your story and His, discover more and to share them with others.

I never intended to write these stories per se. It started one Labor Day. Our family had just returned from a vacation in San Diego and a visit to Sea World. I had just finished reading Donald Miller's *Blue Like Jazz*. I loved His reflections, vulnerability, insight, and non-religious view of Christian spirituality. I rolled from my pillow to my right, and told my wife Karen, "Honey, you've got to read this, it's excellent." Karen has been blessed with an incredibly quick wit. She looked at my bookmark, sticking above the pages, and saw it was my Sea World admission ticket stub with the image of Shamu. She instantly replied, "I'll read *Blue Like Jazz* when it's *Black and White Like Shamu*."

Soon thereafter I sat at our dining room table with a cup of Peet's coffee, a new fountain pen, a journal my wife had given me, and began to write *Black and White Like Shamu* (that story was re-named *The Diver* and is part of this collection of essays). A few hours later, several cups of coffee were consumed, much brown ink had anointed the journal pages, and the story was done. I came to my wife, handed her the journal and said, "Here it is *Black and White Like Shamu*. Now you have to read it."

Karen read the story, was gracious, and encouraged me, "This is pretty good." I shared the stories with some friends at church and they too suggested I share the story with others. Soon thereafter, I had shared the story at the church on a Wednesday night before a couple hundred people. After telling the story at church, the

Wednesday night group talked about some of the themes of the story. We considered: the fears and excitement of beginning a relationship with God, the desire to go deeper, and the truth that God is *not* simply black and white. During that evening I realized that stories will resonate with people and can stir them to grow in God.

BENEFITS **AND BLESSINGS**

There are many benefits and blessings that flow from discovering your story. As I began to write the stories that are collected here, they became an opportunity to reconsider some of the people in my life, their stories and some of my story. One blessing of writing was getting in touch with some of the feelings that I had not considered for a long time. Through that process there was healing. I came to terms with some turmoil and resolved some conflict. In essence, there is personal healing available as you discover your story.

When I started to write *Black and White Like Shamu*, it brought back a sea of memories. I truly reflected upon some of the feelings that I was experiencing at the time. I remembered searching for meaning, and the confusion about who I was, where I was going, and who would be there with me. I could once again *feel* the pain of loneliness, insecurity, and depression. I could almost touch the hole inside of me: the hole that I had once tried to fill with drugs, alcohol, relationships and/or sex.

Writing these stories has been liberating. There is an indescribable freedom associated with discovering your story and sharing it with someone. When I asked Jesus into my life, I experienced a tremendous sense of peace. I felt that the hole inside of me had finally been filled. I was no longer searching for meaning, contentment, or hope. However, I don't really know how much I tried to explore the feelings that I had experienced in the past. Instead I avoided and repressed them. Writing these stories allowed me, at this time in my life, to discover more of those past feelings. In the process I have experienced more of the freedom that Jesus intended for us.

When I began to write the story *Lost and Found*, I wanted so much to show *other* people that there was hope of restoration available in Jesus. What I learned was the amazing healing that I needed and have received in Christ. To confront the feelings that I experienced when I lost my virginity — my innocence — was a place that I had not yet dared venture. To encounter those feelings – some of the shame and pain was uncomfortable to say the least — and then to share those feelings was, at first, frightening. Again, I felt healing when I explored the feelings and freedom when I shared them.

Another blessing was perspective. I was able to see some wonderful people in a new light. We became closer, as I shared my heart with them through story. I think that generally I don't tend to stop and think about how I really feel about people. To take the time to reflect about how I see people in my life and to share those feelings with them was different. I often tell people, "I love you" or "I appreciate you," but to take the time to really dig deeper, and describe the feelings was new. As I shared those feelings with my friends, I discovered that it brought us closer to one another. Similarly, when I shared some of my story with them, it helped us to connect. They could recognize my desire to be vulnerable with them, and that I trusted them and our relationship. I'm confident that the experience has brought us closer.

I also gained some new perspective about myself. Much of that perspective was shared in the stories, but there were also many insights that never made it into the stories. For example, as I was writing the story *One*, I was in East Africa. I was writing about the theme of pride, and how it obscures worship of God and His beauty. Later that day, I asked my friends, who had hosted my visit, if I could leave my clothes behind for someone at the church. They assured me that there was plenty of need, and there were two Sudanese young men (actually Kelli said, "Sudanese boys" but my pride dislikes disclosing the fact that boys would easily fit my "man-size" clothes) who could use the clothes since they were refugees and essentially had nothing. My first thought was that my "nice" clothes should be given to someone who could appreciate them more, and that we could pick-up something "less nice" for the refugees. God immediately struck me right between the eyes with the fact that my heart was wrong, and I was being proud. I felt ugly and ashamed at that moment. The problem of pride that I was describing in the story about another person was revealed in me. The process of story helped to give me new perspective about myself – like a new pair of glasses.

More importantly, through the journey of these stories I gained new perspective on God and my relationship with Him. A new pair of glasses can help you see more clearly, and these times of reflection have helped me to see God more clearly. I love to read the Bible and I love to learn about my God. Learning from the Bible is essential to see God clearly, because it is *His* story. Nevertheless, taking time to discover my relationship with God in the context of these stories has been a new perspective. I've discovered new insight into my relationship with God that has drawn me closer to Him.

An additional blessing I observed was seeing so many of my friends inspired to create. God creates. He even created us in His image. One of those attributes is an ability to be creative. Friends started to write their stories, some painted, and others wrote songs. Being part of a community of people who are released to be creative is exciting. Being creative and sharing that experience with others seems to be contagious. Contaminate others with your creativity, and you'll likely start an epidemic. Stories undoubtedly bring forth more blessings than these. I simply mention a few to stir you to share your stories.

THE **MASTER STORYTELLER**

It might encourage you that I, unfortunately, have no clue about "how to" write. I haven't taken any classes, nor have I received any training. It's not that I'm opposed to receiving guidance; I think it's a great idea. I merely want to help you to see that there are stories inside of you, and it would be great to let them out. Maybe you feel like you're not qualified. Don't worry! I'm no master storyteller either. Yet, I know the Master storyteller.

The reason that we love story is because God loves to communicate through story. The Bible is not only the Word of God, but it is the story of God. We should understand it is a story rather than a list of rules. A story is written by people who want to share their heart with others. Story connects people with one another and connects us with God.

Jesus told parables. A parable is a story that uses comparison, contrast, and analogy to reveal a spiritual lesson or truth. Jesus' parables were told so that we could better understand God. In essence, they were simple stories to help us connect with God.

Great stories have a hook from the start that makes you want to read more. God's story does: "In the beginning, God created the heavens and the earth." When I read that, the first time I opened a Bible, I remember wanting to read more. I recall reading that first verse and thinking, "If God really exists, I want to read the rest of this book, and if He doesn't, then I don't need to waste my time." I decided that I wanted to read more.

God's story continues to unfold, like a great love story, because *it is* the great love story! There is betrayal, jealousy, love, passion restoration, salvation, rescue, and renewal. I love God's story. I marvel that from the very beginning God quickly gives just a snapshot of His creation. In only about a chapter, God tells us about creating the universe: sun, moon, the earth, oceans, trees, plants, birds, fish, land animals, and man. In telling the story, God could have spent seemingly countless words to describe all of creation. But it seems that God wanted to simply provide some context to introduce the main character – man.

Soon we meet Adam and Eve, and then God tells us that He would spend time with them daily. God is telling us very early in the story that it is a love story — His love for us. God creates man with free will, in essence the ability to choose. God loves Adam and Eve, and He gives them the choice to love Him, too. So, God gives them freedom, and just one rule: Don't eat of the tree of the knowledge of good and evil. God's boundaries are always intended to protect us, to bless us and to test our love for Him.

Early in the story, man fails the test. Man forsakes God's perfect love, and eats of the fruit. Immediately, man is separated from God – sin has entered the world. Then, God seeks to begin restoration. God calls to man, beckoning Him to realize his separation from God and God's desire to have relationship with Him.

Through the rest of the story, God faithfully demonstrates and communicates His desire for relationship with us. Adam and Eve, Noah, Abraham, Isaac, Jacob, Joseph, Moses, Joshua, the Hebrew people, Samson, Ruth, Samuel, David, Solomon, Esther and Daniel are all real people with real stories. They are all part of God's story.

Joseph, Mary, the wise men, the shepherds are all real people who bear witness to the birth of Jesus, the focus of all of God's story. He becomes particularly clear to us in the New Testament. The disciples, Nicodemus, the woman at the well, and Paul are all real folks, with real stories and they are all part of God's story. They and others, and you and me, are all chapters in God's story. The story tells the twists, turns, trials, tragedies, and triumphs of people. It seems that the whole thing is a love story.

THE **NEXT CHAPTER**

I've discovered that God's story continues and intersects with my story. My relationship with Him and with others is all part of a great story. When we discover that connection, and share our stories I'm sure it pleases God. I'm also confident that sharing our stories with one another will bring us closer to God as well as one another. I'm not sure what the next chapter will be. This story (or these stories), seems to end here, but really this is just another chapter in a story that is not yet finished. I believe there is plenty of ink left in the fountain pen, so to speak, and that God has more chapters in my story that are left to be discovered, recorded, and perhaps shared. God shares His story, and I suppose we should share ours, too.

I hope that you will be inspired to express your story – your thoughts and emotions – your heart. The psalmist began his song of adoration, "My heart overflows with a beautiful thought! I will recite a lovely poem to the king, for my tongue is like the pen of a skillful poet (writer)" [Psalm 45:1 NLT]. I pray that you also let your heart overflow in a tangible way. Perhaps you'll write in a journal, a poem, a song, or maybe a painting so that others can experience your story and God's story.

Through the journey, I expected to help others come to know Him or to grow in Him. I hope that purpose has been accomplished. What I didn't expect was the personal growth that I experienced in the process. This journey has been one of the best experiences in my life with Jesus.

One of the most important lessons, that I hope to carry into the next chapter of my life, was discovered along this journey. In each of our lives there is an orientation toward task or relationship. Some of us are very task-oriented and can accomplish many things. We love to live life in a sense that every day presents challenges that can be recorded on a "to-do" list. We have great joy in completing tasks and checking them off the list. Task people are more interested in completing tasks than relationships with people. Others are more oriented toward relationship. They have discovered that the greatest value is to be found in connecting with people and developing meaningful relationships.

Jesus is the only one who had a perfect balance between task and relationship. He truly connected with people and modeled authentic relationship. Yet, He also accomplished all the Father had sent Him to do. Jesus did just the right amount of task so that nothing that He was supposed to do was left undone, and He had the wisdom not to seek to do more than He was supposed to. By attaining balance regarding task, He was available for relationship. He invested time with people to develop relationships, and it paid huge dividends. It brought Him joy and satisfaction, and there were immeasurable blessings for the countless lives He has touched and still touches.

As we consider our lives, most of us are oriented clearly toward task or relationship. Only a relatively small percentage of us are so extreme in our orientation that it would appear to be at a polar extreme. Therefore, most of us see ourselves as pretty balanced or close to the middle. In reality, we are not as close to the middle as we think. In the process of this journey, I discovered the importance of relationship in a new light.

I tend to be oriented toward task more than relationship. Along the way, I was moved toward the center. I learned about the beauty of relationship – my relationship with God and with others. It seems only appropriate, as I write the concluding thoughts of this book, that I'm sitting at a familiar table in Nairobi, Kenya. I have written at this table before, and been moved by God in this place. But the poignant timing relates to the Kenyan people. Their culture is so very relationship-oriented. Here, there is a spirit of *karibu* – a welcoming hospitality. Task takes a backseat to relationship: it is beautiful to observe and more beautiful to experience.

I discovered that the most beautiful part of the journey is relationship with God and with others. Ironically, healthy relationships can appear to be a huge task, but it's merely a wise investment. Relationships take energy, but unhealthy relationships (or no relationships) ultimately require more – they seem to drain your life. Jesus understands the need for balance and modeled perfect balance between relationship and task for us. He seemed to accomplish so much in and through relationships. Perhaps that is why Jesus was able to distill the essence of the journey: You shall love the Lord, your God, with all of your heart, all of your mind, and all of your soul; and you shall love your neighbor as you love yourself. That is the essence of a life worth living. Enjoy the journey!

ACKNOWLEDGEMENTS

Thanks to you the reader for investing your precious time in reading this book. I hope that God has used this book to draw you closer to Him. We're all discovering our stories, and Lord willing, we'll learn to share them with one another. I have been blessed with a life worth living, not because of things accomplished, things possessed or any other thing. My greatest wealth is the incredibly beautiful people in my life. Thanks for proving to me in such a tangible way that it's all about relationship with God and others. Much love to you all and thanks for letting me share part of your stories.

My wife, Karen, continues to be the godliest woman I know — an observation I had made before our first date. Since then I have had the privilege of meeting countless godly women, but Karen continues to shine as the most precious gem. She is a tremendous wife, an exceptional mom, and the perfect helpmate – an awesome gift from God. I look forward to many more chapters together.

Our sons, Joshua and Jonathan have continued to inspire me as they discover their own stories and God's story. They seemingly have so many chapters yet to be written in their young lives. I have loved their story so far and look forward to seeing God's story unfold in their lives. Thanks to my family for your sacrifice in allowing me the time to write, and the encouragement to continue.

To the staff at Calvary Chapel Camarillo, you're the best friends I could imagine. As you've discovered, each of you is mentioned in at least one chapter. These reflections merely provide a cameo and unfortunately a limited introduction of you to readers. Yet those who know you have discovered your beauty, your love for Jesus, and your kindness, mercy and compassion for people. In a word [or perhaps a pseudo-word], you're the "bestest." Special thanks to Lynn, Armando, and Robb for graciously reading each story and providing great insights, and helpful critique. Your encouragement and the ability to speak the truth in love is a gift from God.

To my church family, I consider it a pleasure to serve God with you and grow together in Him. It is a wonderful experience to enjoy a community of people learning to love a perfect God and one another. I am frequently amazed at the transforming work that I see God doing in so many lives, and the influence that He makes in us and through us. It is a blessing to worship with people who accept and love others. Thank you for the love, support, and trust you have shown me.

Once again, I want to thank the "commakazes" Armando Garza, Seana Dawson, and Kristina Krikes for all their help and editing assistance. If there are any mistakes I assume full responsibility as I likely inadvertently neglected one of your corrections to the manuscript. Ironically, there were no doubt grammar errors that you corrected in my acknowledgement to you and others. Thanks for your great attention to detail and helping the story flow.

Eric, you are so creative and such a blessing in my life. The cover and book layout, as usual, are inspired and inspiring. Thanks for creating a look that makes the book! Rich, thanks for taking the manuscript and preparing the text for print. It's hard to believe that this was our seventh book together. You continue to bless my life.

To my bro Seth: heartfelt thanks for sharing so much of my story with me [especially the first 17 years in the same apartment]. Undoubtedly you have a unique perspective on our life, and you brought a different perspective to the book that enhanced this work. It is true what the Bible says, "A brother is born to help in time of need" [Proverbs 17:17]. I love you!

Wayne and Clay Jacobsen were gracious and kind to provide excellent and distinguished insight as experienced writers. They have published several great books that have blessed me and many others, and have helped many to grow in their relationship with God. You can check out Wayne's resources and books at: www.lifestream.org. Clay's books are available at: www.clayjacobsen.com.

I was also inspired by my friends on a recent trip to Nairobi, Kenya. Ed and Kelli, thanks for the work that you do for God and His people in Nairobi. I love and admire you and am always blessed by our time together. Tom, thanks for going back with me and blessing our whole team with your leadership. Burt, J.B., Kristina ["Double-K"] and Shirley, it was great to serve and safari with you and to discover our stories together. Shirley, the hand-blown glass beads you made look beautiful on the book cover. To get a better look at Shirley's incredible handmade jewelry visit: www.shirleyjudy.com.

Jesus, thanks for a life worth living. You are the only one worthy to be worshiped. Thanks for helping me to discover You, Your story, and my story, I love You Lord!